contents

introduction

rags, riches, repeat. . . . The course of synthesizer music in the late twen-
tieth century was like a rollercoaster ride from hell. A course where heroes
were born, celebrated, vilified, and then resurrected. It was the best and worst
of times, with seldom a dull moment. But through it all, an elite group of artists
churned out consistently great music that inspired and influenced the masses.
Seventeen of those groundbreakers are profiled in these pages, as are ten key
instruments on which they plied their trade.

For those lucky enough to witness the synth revolution firsthand, the following
paragraphs should strike familiar chords. But for those who are just plugging
in, here's a brief look back at an unforgettable era.

It was the 1970s, and punk and disco were raging from pole to pole. But in
Dusseldorf, Germany, a band called Kraftwerk defied trends by fusing analog synth
bleeps, blips, and vocoded vocals into a stark precision product — and they did
so mostly with hand-built instruments. Meanwhile, in other parts of Europe and
on other continents, there was a groundswell of activity from pioneering artists
such as Brian Eno, Tangerine Dream, Wendy Carlos, Larry Fast, and Isao Tomita.
Synth music was alive and growing, especially in Detroit, where Juan Atkins

and a team of like-minded visionaries (Kevin Saunderson, Rick Davis, Derrick May, Kenny Larkin) were unleashing a new brand of funky techno.

Later in the decade, disco transformed into something called house, thanks to savvy Chicago DJ/producers such as Farley Jackmaster Funk, Jesse Saunders, and Frankie Knuckles, who used analog synths, drum machines, reel-to-reels, and razor blades to bring new energy to the dance floor. Local heroes, yes. International household names, not quite. But artists in the electronic underground were about to get their mainstream due thanks to a potent delivery medium called MTV.

In the 1980s, as the video revolution spread like a virus, such synth-based bands as Depeche Mode, Duran Duran, The Human League, Erasure, and Gary Numan mounted a second British invasion. Haircuts, eyeliner, Spandex, and synthesizers . . . fashion collided with music like never before, and the global youth bought in big time.

All was well on the synthesized front until the early 1990s, when a steamroller named grunge came onto the scene. Forget keyboards, the era was all about guitars and goatees. Seattle was the vortex, and home to the biggest bands in the land: Nirvana, Pearl Jam, Soundgarden, Alice In Chains.

Synths weren't dead, though. Down in the underground, punk and metal were colliding with digital, and it was the angriest synthesized sound ever: industrial. Skinny Puppy, KMFDM, Front Line Assembly, Ministry, Nine Inch Nails, and later Marilyn Manson . . . this aggressive genre hit like a wrecking ball, and simply couldn't be ignored.

By the end of the decade, synth music was everywhere — on radios, televisions, and in dance clubs. Styles cross-pollinated, and sub-genres such as acid jazz, trip-hop, jungle, drum 'n' bass, and big beat were born. The Chemical Brothers and Prodigy sold over a million records each. Madonna signed on with ambient pioneer William Orbit to produce the multiplatinum electro-pop smash *Ray of Light*. Cutting-edge ambience wafted into households weekly via composer Mark Snow and the hugely successful *X-Files* TV series. Synths were on top again.

Which brings us to the present, and this book. While not intended to be an all-encompassing historical guide to the past three decades, the following pages are devoted to a group of diverse and influential electronic music ground-breakers. These artists were chosen not only because they made (and continue to make) an indelible mark on their respective scenes, but also because they were generous enough to let their stories be told through the pages of *Keyboard* magazine. Many of their classic interviews are revisited here, along with profiles of related gear. The book closes with a section of high-impact mini-interviews called Filtersweep, and a recommended listening guide compiled by leading musicians, journalists, and music industry icons.

It's my pleasure to present *Electro Shock! Groundbreakers of Synth Music.* I hope you'll enjoy reading it as much as I did putting it together.

GREG RULE

and Product Spotlights

the chemical brothers

Water Into Acid: The Chemical Brothers Blow Up

t race the course of music evolution and you'll find a handful of key historymakers at each link in the chain. From the classical masters to the pop icons of the past few decades, there have always been, and will continue to be, those who rise above their peers and become symbols of an era.

Only time will tell who earns that distinction from today's group, but in the burgeoning world of electronic dance, keep your eye on a pair of young men from England known as the Chemical Brothers. Tom Rowlands and Ed Simons, still in their 20s, have fast become a global phenomenon.

After taking in one of their live shows, it's easy to see why. Fusing elements of techno and hip-hop, and shoving the mix down the throat of a fuzz box, the Chemical Brothers bust through speakers like a brass-knuckled fist. Their sound is hard, rough, and relentless, and it boils with energy and attitude. In a music market still coming to grips with the return of synths to the mainstream, this English package is a most welcome arrival.

How did the Chemicals get their start? Like many great partnerships, Rowlands and Simons came from two disparate yet complementary musical camps. "I

When Ed Simons (L) and Tom Rowlands started dropping funky breaks in the early '90s, they were known in the U.K. as the Dust Brothers. But a conflict with the popular American production team of the same name forced them to change Dust to Chemical. The album *Exit Planet Dust* was released, and the rest is history.

◄···························

started on piano when I was eight or nine," Rowlands recalls. "I played the guitar and stuff, and was in bands at school. I always had a drum machine because I liked the fact that I didn't have to rely on anybody else. You could go into the bedroom and have this machine play for you. And then I got a sampler, and suddenly I saw this whole other way of making music, and it seemed so exciting to me."

Rowlands made the fateful connection with sidekick Simons at college. "Ed comes from a totally different background. He wasn't that technical or musically based. He had a more DJ approach, which was a good thing, I reckon. If you have two people who are musically obsessive or technically obsessive, you kind of lose that thing of what's good and what's not. You get so far removed from it."

The duo soon began DJing together, igniting rave after rave, and then one day Ed propositioned Tom. "He asked me, 'What if we made our own records?' I said, 'Well, we can, because I know how to make them.' And it was like that, really."

Talk about getting off to a good start. Their first single, "Song to the Siren," went straight to hitsville. "We made that song in my bedroom on an Akai S1000 and a Roland Juno 106," says Rowlands, "and it was mastered on a Hitachi hifi. You can't believe how we made that record then. At the time it was just a rough idea, but I think it came across quite well — that DIY [do it yourself] kind of thing. And that's the good thing about this kind of music: It can be made, and you don't need all this great equipment, and you don't need to be a band rehearsing and gigging around the country. You can just go to your bedroom and make it."

Make it they did.

I exchanged handshakes with the Chemicals backstage at the Organic festival in late '96, but Tom and Ed weren't in the interviewing mood at the time. When they proceeded to knock my block off later that night with their awesome live set, and then again three months later in San Francisco, I knew this story was worth chasing. Eight months later, the chance to roll tape with the Brothers finally came when they visited New York in early '97.

Brother, actually. Since Tom is the half who likes to talk gear and techniques, and since Ed was doing his best to appease a hungry flock of press vultures, I went one-on-one with Tom, who took me behind the scenes in the studio and onstage.

chemical cookbook

Your sound has been described as a hybrid of techno and hip-hop. Is that a fair assessment?

Well, when we started DJing together, Ed and I hit upon this idea of making records that combined, yeah . . . techno and hip-hop, which no one had really done to its fullest extent, we thought. And that's been the basic premise for our records — this combination of things. And now, I think we've taken that quite far, and we're just going off in different things.

Has your method of making music changed much since *Exit Planet Dust*?

On a basic level, it's that we've had more time and flexibility. I think the difference between the two records is the way we've treated sounds. We were getting into it on the first record, but I think we spent a lot longer just messing around with the sound, and having longer to work on specific things, really, whereas before, the songs were made quicker.

Brothers gonna work it out. . . . The Chemicals caught in the live act at San Francisco's Warfield theater during their 1997 *Dig Your Own Hole* tour.

> ## "When we started DJing together, Ed and I hit upon this idea of making records that combined techno and hip-hop, which no one had really done to its fullest extent, we thought. And that's been the basic premise."

Describe the environment you recorded in?

We have our own little studio set up around a Mackie 8-bus and a pair of DynAudio N2s with the ABS Sub Bass system. Just a little project studio where we write, and some things we record onto a Hi8 [TASCAM DA-88] 8-track. If we like the sound we get in there, then we use it. But generally for the more complicated tracks where there's more stuff going on, we go downstairs. Our studio is based in this complex in Southeast London, a place called Orinoco. We have our room upstairs, and they have a proper studio downstairs with a big Neve console. So we mix on that.

Does the process typically begin with a drum loop?

No real method, really. A lot of the tracks do start off with. . . . We'll hear an interesting little snare sound, or an interesting loop, and we'll take it. We use [Steinberg] ReCycle a lot, and that's one thing, on a technical level, that's made our life easier. We used to spend a lot of time chopping up breaks by hand. Like, we'd do a remix for someone, and the first day-and-a-half would usually be spent chopping up breaks and making them fit and groove. And now the program does it for us, which is brilliant. So that's been a big advancement for us — the ease of being able to chop up breaks like that.

Is vinyl your main source for loops and samples?

Yeah. I mean, we'll hear things, sample it, play around with it, and start adding our own stuff to it. A lot if it is actually me playing guitar and bass on the record. And then some tracks, like the last two, are written around a guitar and a sitar, which I played, and then we made a loop out of it. But generally,

I like the sound you get when you sample things from all different contexts and put them together. You end up with a sound that you can't get any other way. You're sampling from eight completely different sources, and they've all been treated differently, and you put them all together.

manglers

You've become masters at murdering sounds.

Yeah. We don't make clinical machine music, even though I'm a great fan of bands like Kraftwerk and such where everything is so precise. I really like that. But one of the major things we've done from the beginning is use rough guitar effects. We've got quite a large collection of Electro-Harmonix pedals and stuff like that. They always put a bit of a bite into things, which you don't really get from your new, latest Roland effects unit type of thing. I think when people were making effects and pedals back then, there was a wild edge to what they were doing. I think it was more experimental.

Is there one particular pedal that gets the most service?

The [Electro-Harmonix] Bass Microsynth, which is quite a fierce pedal. And we use the Frequency Analyzer a lot, which has got the wildest filter I've ever heard. It's the most extreme thing. I was reading some literature about it the other day, and it was meant to be used on brass. I can't imagine any horn player playing through it. [*Laughs.*] If you put a bass through it, or drums, it just sounds wild.

It's funny how some of the most popular equipment was originally intended to serve a completely different purpose. Roland's TB-303, for example. I'm sure the engineers never imagined it becoming the defining voice of trance.

I know. Whoever thought that was going to mimic proper bass . . . it's just amazing. I mean, if that was intended to replicate a bass player, then why are the filters so extreme?

How did you get that roaring sound in the song "Setting Sun"?

It's a composite sound. We'd gotten this ARP system [the 2600], and we were spending a lot of time making those big boom kick drum sounds. And so we got this sound that was really just a block. It didn't have a quick release. It was just more of a [*sings*] *bwwoooooh* sound. Then we started mixing it up with some other sounds,

"One of the major things we've done from the beginning is using rough guitar effects. We've got quite a large collection of Electro-Harmonix pedals and stuff like that. They always put a bit of a bite into things."

little stabs and stuff. Then we put it in the E-mu [e-64] and started messing around with the filters. Out popped this really percussive, rumbling sound. The metallic effect that kind of spirals down is my guitar going through an amp, miked up, and feeding back through a Roland Space Echo. I was just messing around with the rate.

What's your take on the new crop of synthesizers?

Too many machines today are boring. This idea of having to replicate the sound of, I don't know, a great piano or whatever. I mean, if you want that, get the real thing. For us, synthesizers are for making sounds that no other machines can make — not for copying other sounds. It's all about making sounds that no one has ever heard before. It's an exciting thing, and it gives the records an edge. I mean, we spend hours. . . . We've got an ARP 2600, and we spend days playing around with it. I like that kind of thing.

What about the new virtual analog synths?

I remember speaking to Underworld a while ago, and they had just gotten one of the [Clavia] Nord Leads. They were saying how amazing it was. But we haven't bought any of those things yet. No [Korg] Prophecy or Nord or any of those, and I don't know quite why that is, because I'm sure if I did buy one I'd be quite impressed. Part of it is me being wary of mass-produced. . . . Everyone is going out and buying the Prophecy, and everyone is going out and buying the Nord Lead. It's cool, and I'm sure I'm hearing those noises on records and thinking they're good, but I suppose I'm more interested at the moment in. . . . The

"Too many machines today are boring. This idea of having to replicate the sound of, I don't know, a great piano or whatever. I mean, if you want that, get the real thing. For us, synthesizers are for making sounds that no other machines can make — not for copying other sounds."

most exciting piece of equipment we've got at the moment is the ARP 2600. We're really getting into that. It's not very controllable, but some of things you can come up with are wicked. And we've also got this guy in Germany who's made some things for us. He makes these things called Shermans: the Sherman Filter Bank and the Sherman Chaos Bank. He only makes, like, 50 of each of them, and they're just wild. They sound really good. Extreme.

What does the Chaos Bank do?

[*Laughs.*] It's a little modular synth setup, and it comes out with the most unearthly noises. I think he's building a big modular system, and I think this is one part of it. It's worth checking out.

And you're sampling maniacs, of course.

For ages we've been using Akai samplers, and just recently we went out and bought the new E-mu range. We're just getting into that — into the synthesis/sampling engines of those machines. Just the way you can patch things together where the LFO is controlling the start point of the sample. Stuff like that. A lot of our sounds are done through that cross-patch page in the E-mu. A really good way of working.

You mentioned using ReCycle earlier. What other software programs do you use?

We use [Digidesign] Pro Tools when we compile a record, but the one thing I'd like to get into more is having the ease of moving large chunks of music around. At the moment what we do, is . . . a lot of the things on the record are quite sectional. They were recorded at different times, because we wanted to get that feel of certain old records where things were edited together from different takes. Say a Beatles record, or whatever: You can hear a completely different sound from section to section. So what we were doing was recording sections. We'd do, like, two days recording a track, put it on a DAT, and then work another two days on the same track with a totally different setup. And then without Pro Tools, what we did was use our large sampler arsenal to put a lot of the information in, and then play with it as if it were loops. It is quite cool, because you get that feeling as if it were different records being cut together, when in fact it is your own music. It's quite a laborious process 'cause you've got to make the equivalent of like four records to get it.

Once all of the loops and pieces were stored in your samplers, how did you control them?

We use [Steinberg] Cubase on a Mac. We've got an [Akai] MPC3000 as well, which we sometimes use for the feel of it. It's good to be able to hit things [*referring to the MPC's front-panel trigger pads*]. We only got the MPC about a year and a half ago to basically play live with. But then when we started playing live with it, we realized the things you can do with it that you can't do with a computer. Being able to bash the pads. . . . In fact, one thing I want to get is that E-mu Launch Pad thing, which looks quite cool. Having real-time controllers, and a fader, is quite cool for us. It's a DJ kind of thing, because you have the fader controlling the volume and stuff.

When using effects, do you try to perfectly match the delays with the bpm of the song, for example, or is it more a feel process?

It's just whatever feels right. I mean, I can never find my bpm tempo chart. It just doesn't matter, really. Sometimes I'll set the Roland [Space Echo] delays, and you get a loose kind of feel. The way we make drum loops move, the way we put movement into them, is to put a lot of little short delays on them, and then play around with the delay times. And then when you get everything grooving together, you record it. As long as it sounds good, that's all that matters.

Chemical Brother
Tom Rowlands
digs into the
decks. The Bro-
thers started
out as DJs, and
later transitioned
into making their
own tracks.

thieves?

Much continues to be said about the legalities of sampling from other artists. What's your view on this issue?

Our approach, especially on this record, is to disguise it. We like the idea of the sample culture. In the late '80s you had those records where people were just bare-faced stealing, things like De La Soul and stuff. I thought it was quite a liberating thing. I really liked it. You could sit these things next to each other, and people knew what they were. But the thing is, you can't do that now, really. And so, since we've been making records . . . the main thing is to take a source sound and make it something else that it wasn't. You start with a sound that you generally know, and think is cool, and then you move it some-where else. And we cut it up so small. If you play the things we've sampled to the people who played them, they wouldn't be able to tell it was them. That's an exciting thing. I like the feeling of having a recorded sound, and in essence, you're recording it again. You know, someone took it that far, and now you're taking it somewhere completely different. And when you start mixing up different things, you end up with things that you'd never think of. It's a good way of working.

showtime

What's your approach to recreating your recorded music on the concert stage?

Our basic view is that when we play live, we strip things down. We get rid of a lot of stuff that's on the record. When we play, we want people to dance, and get locked into that thing. So what we do, the actual nuts and bolts of it, is we loop up lots of our tracks. We have three samplers — an Akai MPC3000, an E-mu e64, and an Akai S3000 — which are all fully expanded. And on those, we have loops of our songs that we've made up at home. And then we have the MPC3000 running in sync with a TASCAM DA-88.

What material do you keep on tape?

More of the treated-type stuff that we haven't got enough sample space for. So what we do is, both are in sync, and we cut between stuff on the sequencer and stuff on the DA-88, which for us is quite a flexible way of working. I mean, a lot of times the DA-88 is just muted. If we're on the bus that afternoon, and we have the idea of extending a section, we can just extend it in the MPC. For us, that's the exciting thing about making the music live. And it's something that's really shaped the way we make records. It is a testing ground, so to speak. It is a place where you can try out different things.

How is the data organized?

In the MPC we have "bands" — programs in the samplers — that all correspond to a particular bpm. This band is 120 bpm, and then there will be a definite point in the sequence where the bpm changes. Maybe it gets knocked down to 111, or up to whatever. So we have loads of loop-groups of our tracks that all work at these bpms. And basically us playing live is cutting between different stuff of ours, or remixes we've done, or anything we can load into the sam-

"One thing about electronic bands who play live: They always feel this pressure to take 'real musicians' onstage. That wouldn't work for us because that's not how we make music. Even when we bring in live musicians, or when we play stuff on the tracks ourselves, we always, always loop the things up and get them in the sampler and treat them that way. That's when we're happiest — doing things that you couldn't physically do."

pler that afternoon. If it's at that bpm, then we can flip in whatever. Then, along with that, on the MPC we have loads of keyboard lines and stuff running through to, like, the Juno 106.

What drew you to the MPC as your primary live sequencer?

It's a great thing to have live 'cause you can just jam on it. It's cool. After playing live with it, you come back and sit in front of the computer, and you lose a bit of that intuitive thing. You can't hit it. [*Laughs.*] But then there's other parts of it that I find really annoying. I've been brought up in [Steinberg] Pro24 and Cubase and I have to see the songs, and like that, especially with complicated arrangements. It gets quite difficult. But then live, when you're just working in blocks of bpms, it's quite easy.

Is there a certain approach you take each night in terms of the bpm sequence?

We have a variety of sequences that we programmed at home, so we can say, "What do you fancy tonight?" That type of thing. But generally, we spend a lot of time sorting out what we're going to do. We know in each section . . . I'm in control of the sequencer, and Ed knows that if I go into a certain section, he'll know what's coming up next and can change the patches and stuff on the Juno. The thing is, we've made music so long together, and we've DJed so long together, that it's quite locked in, really. That's one thing about electronic bands who play live: They always feel this pressure to take what people refer to as "real musicians" onstage. That wouldn't work for us because that's not how we make our music. Even when we bring in live musicians, or when we play stuff on the tracks ourselves, we always, always loop the things up and get them in the sampler and treat them that way. That's when we're happiest — doing things that you couldn't physically do. We like the way it sounds. Someone once said to us, "Why don't you get a live drummer?" And we said, "No. The drums we use are not physically reproducible."

Leave that stuff to Jack Dangers, eh?

Exactly, which he does quite well. But we're just on another tip, really. We like machines. We like that control you have.

Live drummer or not, there's no lack of energy on your stage. You both seem to wring the notes out of your machines.

Yeah, it's cool. Our music is exciting, and that's the spirit of it. That's why it's good to play it live. You can crank it up, and that's how people should hear it — and in a room with a load of other people who are having a good time. A lot of our songs are based around that kind of feeling. And then when you get to play it live, it's a really good feeling. How can we not get into it?

Your setup is a pile of gear and spaghetti-like wiring — a bit dangerous-looking, actually. Any disasters to report?

[*Laughs.*] Yeah, we've had a few. Nothing really that bad, but a few nights when the DA-88 wouldn't work. Moisture and stuff. But, luckily, we're flexible, so we can just play off the MPC.

Unless it crashes.

Yeah, it's a difficult thing to take these pieces of equipment, which are fine in the studio but don't do so well when they get sweaty and dirty. It is quite a testing thing. The MPC, one time, got smashed up coming through the airport. It was a mad scramble around to get stuff. We use SyQuest 270s [removable hard-disk cartridges], and all our stuff is on that. I suppose we're a bit foolish for not having DAT backups, but we don't. I think we'll get more safety-conscious on the next tour, but we've always managed to get through. People don't understand. They think, "Ah, you're using machines, nothing goes wrong." But if you've got a band, and, say, the bass drum mic gets knocked over or something, at least you've got a lead singer who can tell a few jokes — or do an acoustic set. But with us, if someone kicks out the power, we're looking at a major disaster.

We did this gig once supporting the Prodigy. [Singer] Keith Flint came out when we were playing "Chemical Beats," and he started dancing around our stack, and knocked out the power lead to the mixer. Suddenly there was nothing. That was probably the worst moment we've had onstage.

How is the sound handled at your live shows — do you send a stereo feed to the house?

Most of the time, yeah, because the real integral part of the performance is how we're mixing it. So all we send out is a left and a right, and some different effects output auxiliaries and stuff. The guy who does our front of house plays around with it, and all he has to do is make sure it's loud enough and that the general EQ is okay. A lot of the soundcheck is spent making sure everything sounds right. We know how things sound through our little Sennheiser headphones, so we try to get the monitors as close as we can to that.

When we did a tour in England, we were able to get a big sound system that had Pink Floyd's old desk out front, and a jog wheel for rotating sound around. So for that we sent out lots of different things. Delays were colliding around the room, and stuff. Pretty cool.

exit

Your collaboration with Noel Gallagher was an interesting and successful venture. Where do you see the Chemical Brothers heading in the future?

I'm sure the record company would like us to do more of that, but we've done that now, so. . . . Obviously we'll continue to collaborate with people because it's something we enjoy doing, and it's good when people bring different things to the sound. We like that, and that's why we enjoy doing remixes: getting to jam with other people's ideas, and putting your own twist into them. But we don't want to get into that thing that a lot of techno people tend to get into when they're making records, which is, "We need to have a voice on this song," or "We need to have this element on this song." And they end up with an album full of collaborations. You're left thinking, "Whose record is this?" But there are no hard and fast rules. If someone comes to us next week and says, "Do you fancy doing this?" and it's a good idea, then sure. Why not?

[by Greg Rule, Keyboard, June 1997]

arp 2600

he ARP Instrument Company introduced its line of high-tech analog modular synthesizers, the 2500 series, in 1970. These instruments featured matrix-switch patching (no "patch-cord jungle") and stable oscillators. ARP's founder, Alan R. Pearlman, recognized the importance of teaching musicians how to use the technology, so he designed a new instrument with a fixed selection of basic synthesizer functions. This instrument, dubbed the Model 2600, was an integrated system with the signal generating and processing functions in one box and the keyboard in another. The functionality was borrowed from the original ARP modules, but instead of using matrix-switches (which were expensive and bulky) for patching, Pearlman devised a system of factory-installed "normal" connections between the modules. These connections could be added to or replaced by patch cords. Thus, a beginning user could work the system relatively simply. When the user desired to develop more complex sounds, patch cords could be added as needed.

vital stats

Description: Patchable monophonic analog synthesizer (two-voice polyphonic keyboard after 1975).
Production Dates: 1970-1981
Manufacturer: ARP Instruments, Newton and Lexington, MA (out of business).
Original Price: $3,600 from 1975 to 1981. (Price unavailable for pre-1975 model.)

Pearlman believed that schools with small or medium-sized music departments were the main market for this new instrument. To further enhance

The ARP 2600. Originally targeted at schools, this instrument became a staple of synth-based pop, rock, experimental, and, eventually, modern dance music.

the 2600's educational value, Pearlman put graphics on the console's front panel so the signal paths were easy to follow, and used sliders and slide switches so the control and switch settings were easy to see. The first production run had blue panels, painted sheet-metal cases, and polished wood handles. "That's not what I wanted," Pearlman recalls. "I wanted the instrument to be housed in a rugged case that would travel safely. But those were the days when nobody would listen to you if you were over 30, so the young designer had his way." Musicians and retailers, however, quickly shot down the "Blue Marvin" or "Blue Meanie" design in favor of the vinyl-covered luggage-style case with the dark gray panel that remained in production from 1971 to 1981.

Edgar Winter was the first high-profile musician to pick up on the 2600. He had the keyboard equipped with a long extension cord, which enabled him to wear the keyboard around his neck like a guitar. Pete Townshend, who also had a 2500 modular system, was another early 2600 user. Stevie Wonder had the control panel of his 2600 labeled in Braille.

A couple of years after the 2600 was introduced, Tom Oberheim came out with a kit that would convert the 2600 into a two-voice instrument. The kit worked by converting the keyboard so it would produce both high-note and low-note voltages. Since the instrument had three oscillators, you could use one or two of the oscillators for the high note, and another oscillator or two for the low note.

In 1975, ARP incorporated Oberheim's idea into its standard production models. The keyboard circuitry was redesigned to include not only the two-voice mode, but also delayed vibrato, interval latch, single and multiple trigger, and improved pitch-bend capability. The new keyboard had the model number 3620, whereas monophonic keyboard model numbers were 3601 and 3604. (The console model number was always 2600.)

The 2600 color scheme remained black, gray, and white until 1978, when the look of the entire ARP product line was changed. After 1978, the panel graphics were white and orange, and the panel itself became a darker gray.

ARP ceased operations in 1981.

[by Bob Moog, Keyboard, October 1989]

william orbit and madonna

The Methods and Machinery behind Madonna's *Ray of Light*

from the original underwear-clad party girl to the all-black and tattooed Veronica Electronica in the "Frozen" video, Madonna has made an indelible time-stamp on history with her ever-changing fashion and musical sensibilities. Some of her expeditions have mined more gold than others, but she really hit the nail on the head with *Ray of Light* (Maverick). Gone for the most part are the sex-me-up lyrics and sugar-pop productions. The lyrics reflect a first-time mother's emotional and spiritual growth, and the productions are stunning . . . a masterful mix of spiky synths, chopped samples, and stark orchestration. Just as Björk did with Mark Bell on *Homogenic*, Madonna met her magical match in producer/songwriter William Orbit.

Followers of experimental electronic music will need no introduction to William. He's been breaking boundaries in the ambient underground for years. His *Strange Cargo* series laid the groundwork for countless modern electronic artists, and his remix list reads like a Who's Who of rock and pop. (For a

William and his workhorse: the Korg MS-20. Orbit's electronic magic on Madonna's *Ray of Light* helped earn the pop queen four awards at the 1999 Grammies.

◀ ··························

deeper look into Orbit's past, visit the many online archives devoted to his exhaustive body of work.)

I was invited to spend an afternoon at Orbit's home studio in 1998 . . . a treat, to say the least. He was remodeling on the day of the interview, so gear was piled waist-high and from end to end. It was my first encounter with William, so I didn't know quite what to expect. Born and bred in England, would he fit the typical British I'd-rather-not-reveal-how-I-make-my-music mold?

Turned out he was anything but tight-lipped, or ordinary. William's a bit of a rare bird. He's tall, lanky, gap-toothed, and has a set of quirky, rubbery facial expressions that demand your attention. A genuine character, and with no detectable negative attitude, William was as warm and gentlemanly as they come. But best of all for us keyboard types, he's a veritable gold mine of electronic music know-how. Years after his entry into the international music scene, he remains on the leading edge of the experimental curve, and is as vital now as ever.

"William is a complete madman genius," according to Madonna. "I'd come to him with an idea of where I wanted to go musically, hum melodies or read lyrics, and then leave him alone in the laboratory. Sometimes he'd go in the direction I wanted and sometimes he'd swerve off somewhere else entirely. We'd end up with trance tracks that were eight minutes long and then keep adding and subtracting until we had real verses and choruses. We really put our noses to the grindstone."

Madonna was quoted on VH-1 as saying she'd always been interested in techno music, but felt that it generally lacked emotion. Working with Orbit, she hoped to "prove that it could be emotional." We'd say she succeeded. When asked if there was a clearly defined concept going into the project with William, she said, "No, that evolved when we got together and started writing." Her early brainstorming sessions with William were "like discovering an old, long-lost friend." Madonna was a fan of his past work, which included remixes from her *Erotica* album.

Star artists often keep tight control over their producers. When asked how much creative latitude Madonna allowed Orbit in the studio, she revealed, "William

"He's a complete madman genius," says Madonna of her *Ray of Light* collaborator, William Orbit.

had a very long leash, but I was firmly holding on to the end of it." Her analogy of the process: "I was the anchor, he was the waves, and the ship was our record."

Despite the fact that William Orbit has been on more records than an average musician would in a dozen lifetimes, he was as passionate about the *Ray of Light* release as if it were his first. "I don't mind talking about it at all," he enthused. "I was so involved in it. I didn't feel like it was just a gun-for-hire situation. Obviously it was Madonna's record, but I'm as proud of it as if I'd done it myself." When I told him how many spins I'd given the disc by the time of the interview, he smiled and said, "This record is meant to be listened to many times, but the thing I'm pleased about is that it gets some people on the first play. If someone asked me if I preferred to have a record that grabbed people by the balls straight away but became tiresome soon after, versus one that took forever to get into but kept people replaying it, obviously I'd go for the latter. And normally I do. But the downside to that is things often don't ever get heard by anybody that way. The pleasant surprise about this record is that there's an instantness about it, even though it's definitely meant to be played over a period of time. Another funny thing is that there isn't a consensus on the tracks. People will usually agree broadly on which of the songs they prefer, but here there's a real admitted division. There are some tracks that people generally like, like 'Drowned World,' but there are others that polarize opinion, like 'Shanti.' They either play it all the time obsessively or skip it on the CD. There's been quite a lot of dispute, and it's been murder choosing singles."

Here's what William had to say about the making of *Ray of Light,* including how he got the job, how the sessions progressed, and what tools and techniques he used to give Madonna her most mesmerizing sound to date.

Being asked to produce Madonna's new record must have sent skyrockets shooting off in your head. Tell us how you landed this assignment?

I was talking to Guy Oseary, who runs Maverick, and he mentioned that Madonna was looking for material. It just so happened I had a lot of tapes of half-formed ideas lying around, so when he asked me to send some stuff over I was happy to just knock off a DAT with miscellaneous bits on it.

Was the DAT well-received?

I sent it to her and she was back on the phone within five days. She'd already starting writing to it. So we had a long chat, and I could tell straightaway that she was serious. I'm quite guarded about people who might take the tracks and miss the point, but I knew she got it. And so I went out there and we started working on the album.

Describe the material that was on your demo.

Many of the ideas were fairly formed. The germ of, say, "Drowned World," was on that tape, although if you compare it to what you hear on the album you'll hear quite a progression. The germ of "Mer Girl" was on that tape. And so she ran with the ball, threw it back to me, and then for the last stage of the project we worked at Larrabee [Studios in Southern California] in a more conventional way.

When you say "germ," are you talking about backing tracks with no melodies?

Some had melodic lines, but it really was a whole selection of. . . . It ran all the way from complete tracks, really, to just bare-bones backing tracks on which she subsequently put her lyrics and melodies. They were all different, and that's why to me the album sounds quite varied. Some people tell me it's contiguous-sounding, but I hear a lot of stylistic variation. The tracks were done in different ways, which I understand isn't the way Madonna usually works. She normally has a more set approach to making an album. But we didn't have a strict method of working; we changed it all the time.

Were there preliminary demo sessions before you officially started recording?

We met at her house in New York, and she played me some things that she'd worked on with other people. So we were really just getting in sync with each other at that point. Then we booked time at the Hit Factory in New York City later that week, and that was pretty exciting because that was the first time I heard her sing her parts. And so we proceeded to go through the tracks and rough out what we were going to do.

Were all of your keyboards set up in the studio at that point?

No. Everything was mainly on tape. We were focusing on vocals during those sessions. It wasn't until later that I went back to England, packed up my gear, and brought it over.

And what gear was that?

How did I know you would ask me that? Oh, it's not a ton of gear. Most of it is pretty retro: a Korg MS-20, a Roland Juno-106, a Roland JD-800. Much of the album was done on a Juno-106. You can get so much out of that synth. Also, a significant amount of it was done on the MS-20 — the more spiky sounds. A few things that people think are guitar are actually the MS-20. And then there were a few more bits and pieces: a few modules, a Yamaha DX7, a Novation Bass Station, a Roland JP-8000, a lot of Roland stuff. I've always liked Roland stuff.

> **"Much of the album was done on a [Roland] Juno-106. You can get so much out of that synth. Also a significant amount of it was done on the [Korg] MS-20 — the more spiky sounds. A few things that people think are guitar are actually the MS-20."**

I have to say, I don't consider myself a keyboardist at all. You know, I'm a two-fingered virtuoso. Wax pencils play a large part in my keyboard playing. I draw on the keys, and I use them to label what I'm doing — what samples are assigned to what key, and so on. Sequencing plays a large part, obviously.

What sequencer did you use on this record?

I started the whole thing on an Atari ST system with Steinberg Cubase II. I didn't know that was unusual until about two-thirds of the way through, when people would comment on it. At one point the thing even caught fire. Really. Smoke coming out of it. It was like, "What's that smell? Oh, it's burning components." But the funniest memory was Madonna, who doesn't do a lot of keyboard playing, messing around on a keyboard marked up with grease pencils. I mean, picture Madonna, the biggest pop star in the world, playing with this retro gear that you could buy for $50 in the Recycler. Later in the project, when Marius DeVries [of Massive Attack fame] came in to work on a couple of tracks, I was blown away by what he was doing in [Digidesign] Pro Tools. I bought my own system soon after that and now I can't leave it alone. My friends Rico Conning and Damian Wagner were around a lot during the Larrabee sessions doing additional programming work.

Madonna has said in other interviews that this record was painfully slow to make.

[*Laughs*] Indeed. It took a long time to do the album, months. And it wasn't like we were slacking, but there were so many details going in. We actually did

"It took a long time to do the album, months. And it wasn't like we were slacking. We actually did have to work fast, and there were many times when we had to move on. One of Madonna's favorite phrases was: 'Don't gild the lily.' In other words, keep it rough, and don't perfect it too much. It's a natural urge for computer buffs to perfect everything because they can, and we were very wary of that."

have to work fast, and there were many times when we had to move on. One of Madonna's favorite phrases was: "Don't gild the lily." In other words, keep it rough, and don't perfect it too much. It's a natural urge for computer buffs to perfect everything because they can, and we were very wary of that. By perfecting, you can lose the character of it, and she always had an eye out for that.

Let's dissect a couple of songs from *Ray of Light*.

Sure, but it's important to point out that they were all done differently. There's nothing wrong with making albums in a formulated way, but in this instance, it definitely wasn't that way. It was serendipity. At first I was only in there to do a couple of tracks. It wasn't clear that I was going to do the whole album, and that, again, led to the sort of disarray with the way it was conducted.

Throughout the record are pulsing, echoing effects, some very tightly timed and some more loosely attached to the beat — in "Drowned World" [at 4:36 on the *Ray of Light* CD] and "Frozen" [1:57], for example. What's your approach to quantization?

Often I won't quantize at all. I do believe that you can take away. . . . You can make something very unlistenable by quantizing it too much. I play a lot of stuff by hand and don't quantize it, and very often it sounds better that way.

Unquantized rhythms work better when used next to quantized rhythms and vice versa.

One of the drum fills in "Frozen" is extra-expressive, going from what sounds like mallets to hard wooden sticks. [1:54]

One of my friends asked, "Is that the track with the trash cans being kicked about?"

Did you achieve that effect with filters?

Yeah, it's all done with filters.

There are wicked drum fills in "Drowned World" [2:30] and "Sky Fits Heaven" [1:46]. How do you create those — from breakbeats?

I mostly construct them out of little tiny fragments — a little bit of this and that, but they weren't off records. We had a couple of sessions with a drummer in Los Angeles, and it didn't quite work out. But Fergus [Gerrand, whose drumming *does* appear on the CD] is someone I work with all the time; I've worked with him for years. So he came to my house in London and put down a load of drums, which I then threw into my system and chopped up and messed around with. But like I said before, I don't use ReCycle or any of those things. I'm not sure if I want to. I mean, I hear some really good stuff being done with it, but I don't want to date-stamp things too much. I'm very cautious about putting out a record that a year down the line will sound date-stamped. So I'm trying to chart my own course, be it good or bad.

So all of your chopping and editing is done directly onboard the Akai samplers?

My own version of ReCycling, if you will.

When Fergus was recording at your home, was he playing along to your sequences?

He was, but they were rudimentary sequences. Don't forget, the thing with modern recording is that you can work backwards. You can do anything in any order you'd like. It's like editing together a film, shooting the first scene last, etcetera. Any approach you'd like. And Fergus is very good about that kind of thing. He knows that what might end up on the record could be completely different from what he originally played.

In "Sky Fits Heaven," there's a nice half-time version of the main drum pattern. [3:45]

I like messing with time signatures. I'm glad you picked up on that. It's fun. Why stick to the same time signature? Something I was really happy with was on "Mer Girl." That song sounds like it's just an ambient piece of soundscape, but in fact it's got verses, bridges, and choruses. It's more structured than you might think at first listen. And when the fourth verse comes in, there's this bit where it goes into lots of conflicting time signatures on top of each other deliberately. [4:19] I thought I'd try it in a visceral kind of way.

And all of these loops and performances were in your Akai samplers being triggered by Cubase events, correct?

Yeah, but there aren't many loops, you see. Most are made up of quite small bits. But everything was coming out of the Akais. In fact, what I normally do,

Kindred spirits. Writing and recording with William Orbit "was like discovering an old, long-lost friend," says Madonna.

"What I normally do, is . . . I use two S3200s, and ultimately the whole soundscape of the track, apart from the vocals, is coming out of the Akai stereo outs and through a valve compressor."

is . . . I use two S3200s, and ultimately the whole soundscape of the track, apart from the vocals, is coming out of the Akai stereo outs and through a valve [tube] compressor. I'm not used to working with automation, and this is the first time I'd fully used it; we used a J-series SSL. I haven't been north of the faders on an SSL ever until this, but I tried to use the stereo outs of my Akais whenever possible because I like the sound of all that material coming from the same outputs. That's when the magic starts happening — when the sum becomes greater than the parts. If you break everything up too much, you lose that. So whenever possible I like to run the majority of the material through the same outputs, and subsequently route it through the same compressor, or whatever.

What compressor do you prefer?

I usually use Drawmers; they work perfectly, and I like the way they sound.

"Skin" is loaded with expressive pitch-delay effects. [2:30, 3:33]

That was Marius; he and I worked on that one. The bit where it kind of drops down is a looped-up guitar — a guitar phrase, looped up and then pitched up and down again.

How did you get the chopped-up vocal effect in the intro? [0:43]

The vocals are going through a Panscan, a scanning device, on one side only. In fact all the tremolo you hear on the album where it's panning is an old Panscan. The Panscan puts the signal back and forth across the stereo field, but you can speed it up. And if you've just got it on one side, it cuts in and out. It's an analog device — knobs, not a mouse.

When did you commit those types of effects to tape — during mixdown or earlier?

"It's all done in a very analog way. Basically, you have two hands, so you've got ahold of two knobs, and you set it up for that golden spot. Every synth has that little G spot where subtle, slight tweaking of two parameters takes you through a huge range of sound. And then you can pick those best performances and stick them back in the sampler."

I record stuff to tape in a really ad-lib fashion. In other words, I'll get the gear going and just "perform" it to tape. And on a project like this, with 48 or more tracks available, you become quite wasteful. But the key is that I would subsequently go back, load the best bits into the sampler, and further manipulate them. You get the best of both worlds that way. I've been doing that for years; I think a lot of people do that. If people aren't using tape, or some type of recording medium, they should. In other words, anybody who just runs everything through live sequencer patches to DAT runs the risk of not getting that kind of grungy . . . . I heard this interview with Tom Waits and he said something to the effect of, "If you overwork music, if you sterilize it or pasteurize it too much, then all the nutrients get lost." That's what we're talking about here. I believe you get more of that in analog recording. Then you shove your analog bits into your sampler or computer and further manipulate it. Wonderful things can happen. Best of both worlds.

What's that Jetsons-like flying saucer sound in "Skin"? [1:31]

The MS-20 is very spiky like that. Like, if you listen to the track "The Power of Goodbye," that's got lots of little sounds like that in it. The MS-20 is great. I mean, there's something about its transient peaks that are very spiky. And you can make that machine scream. Its filters are very severe.

Are these sounds typically made by triggering one note with a long release, and then working the knobs?

It's all done with the onboard VCO, and it's all done in a very analog way. Basically, you have two hands, so you've got ahold of two knobs, and you set it up for that golden spot. Every synth has that little G spot where subtle, slight tweaking of two parameters takes you through a huge range of sound. And then you can pick those best performances and stick them back in the sampler. I think people who use lots of plug-in programs don't always understand that it's better to start off using different VCOs and things on synths to get your source material, because there's something more "analog" about it. There's something about the curve. The human brain can distinguish ever such a lot of information. The way an analog echo throws its repeat back, for example, and the timing of its repeat versus the way a computer does it. It might be subtle, but we can tell that. That's something that should not be underestimated.

Then there's the art of combining disparate types of sounds. For example, the unexpected Middle Eastern flute riff that appears from time to time in "Skin." [1:58]

That was from Marius's holiday. "Skin" was a track that the three of us worked together on [Orbit, DeVries, and Madonna]. We had fun with that one, and that flute was something Marius recorded at a market while on holiday in Morocco. In fact, at the very end of that track I faded it early because everyone starts clapping at the end of the sequence. It didn't sound right to hear applause at the end. It gave the wrong impression of the track, so I faded it early.

What about the other aspects of working with Madonna — recording vocals, for example?

Madonna's production involvement was a major factor in this record, and it's something that shouldn't be overlooked. She is pretty intense when she's doing vocals, and doesn't go over things a lot of times. It's not like ages and ages of takes. She's in the vocal booth, and stuff happens quickly. I always assumed or thought Madonna was more calculating in the way she did music, but in reality it turns out. . . . There is a level of crafting to get things right, but there's also an element of serendipity. Just letting things happen, and keeping the vibe going. She's quite a vibe merchant — a real viber in the studio.

Another thing about Madonna. I've never met anybody who has more ability to make things happen like she does. Stuff happens, and she makes it happen just by the sheer force of her will.

Was it generally clear to you and Madonna when a track was done and ready to be mixed?

Well, the thing is, sometimes you do a demo mix. . . . "Drowned World" was a demo mix, for example. It wasn't supposed to be a final mix, it was a rough, but it worked and that's what you hear on the record. So in that respect it's the time when you say, "Well, it's not finished, but I don't want to take it any further 'cause it seems to have reached a sort of apotheosis. It's perfect now. Let's not take it any further and risk spoiling it. . . . Don't gild that lily!"

Hopefully this record will inspire people to research your *Strange Cargo* back catalog.

I hope so.

You've been so prolific, yet you're not that old. How do you keep the energy up?

Wheat grass and Jack Daniels.

There have been lots of remixes on the radio. Are you involved in the process?

I know of a Stereo MCs one, and Victor Calderone, who does stuff out of Miami. But there's going to be a lot of mixes going on.

Are you responsible for getting the raw material out to the remixers?

To a point, yeah. I have to be, really, 'cause it's all sitting in my Atari and samplers, and a few tapes here and there.

Now that *Ray of Light* is done, and doing well, what's next on your schedule?

Amongst other things I'll be returning to my *Pieces In a Modern Style* record. It was withdrawn shortly after release last year due to copyright problems, which are now resolved. I did versions of my favorite 20th-century compositions. Composers like Henryk Górecki, Samuel Barber, Erik Satie, and Maurice Ravel.

The delay was a blessing in disguise — I now have the opportunity to add some more pieces.

Will this be an acoustic or electronic project?

Both. I use my usual sound pallet, but in a very understated way, to do these interpretations.

Why do I think we'll be seeing your name on the big screen soon?

Well I *am* here in Hollywood, in Tinseltown, aren't I?

[by Greg Rule, Keyboard, July 1998]

korg ms-20

korg introduced the MS-20 patchable mono synth in 1978. Because the internal circuits were normalized, patch cords weren't required for the unit to make sounds, but the presence of patch points made the machine more versatile and expandable. Its design was similar to the ARP 2600, though it was smaller, less complex, and way cheaper. Along with the venerable Roland Juno-106, the MS-20 is a staple of "the William Orbit sound."

According to Korg's Jerry Kovarsky, "The first version of the MS-20 was a large teaching unit. It was made since synthesis was so new, and many companies felt that having schools teaching the basics of analog synthesis would grow the market. The big MS-20 was first produced around 1977, and around 40 to 50 units were sold. What a rare and vintage synth!" The more streamlined MS-20 that hit the mass market soon after featured two VCOs, two VCFs, two VCAs, two EGs, and audio inputs for processing external sounds.

vital stats

Description: Monophonic analog synthesizer with two VCOs, two VCFs, two VCAs, two EGs, and an audio input. Front panel is divided into a control section and a large patch panel for free creative control of signal paths and module functions.

Production Dates: 1978-1980

Manufacturer: Korg

Approximate Number Made: 20,000

Original Price: $1,650.

The MS-20 prototype was a beastly machine aimed at the education market, but it shrank into the consumer production model shown here.

About the company itself: Korg is currently headquartered in Japan, with branches in the U.K. and the U.S., but their beginnings were humble. According to the company, "Korg's founder, Tsutomu Katoh, was a nightclub proprietor in the early 1960s. Tadashi Osanai, a noted Japanese accordionist, regularly performed at his club using a Wurlitzer 'Sideman' rhythm machine. Osanai, an engineering graduate of Japan's prestigious Tokyo University, was dissatisfied with the Wurlitzer machine. And, certain that he could build a better rhythm machine himself, he convinced Katoh to finance his efforts.

"In 1962, Katoh rented a small facility alongside the Keio railway line where Osanai and four assistants worked on developing a mechanical rhythm machine. The fledgling enterprise was dubbed Keio Electronic Laboratories. The Keio name (pronounced Kayo) was used because of the lab's proximity to the railway line, and because it represented the combination of the first initials of Katoh's and Osanai's names.

"In 1963, Keio introduced its first product: the Disc Rotary Electric Auto Rhythm machine, or DoncaMatic DA-20. While primitive by today's standards, the instrument represented a major breakthrough in its day. By 1966, the company had made the transition from electromechanical technology to solid-state with the introduction of the DoncaMatic DE-20.

"In 1967, Katoh was approached by Fumio Mieda, an engineer who wanted to develop keyboard products. Impressed by Mieda's enthusiasm and talents, Katoh gave him a mandate: Go home and design a keyboard product that we can make and sell. Eighteen months later, Mieda returned to the Keio facility with an organ prototype. Unlike most organs on the market at that time, Mieda's prototype had programmable voice capability like a synthesizer. Fifty were produced and sold under the Korg name, a name which was derived from the combination of the words Keio and Organ.

"In 1973, using many of the basic design concepts of Mieda's organ, the company introduced the Mini-Korg, a monophonic synthesizer. Based on the success of the Mini-Korg, Katoh committed substantial resources to the development of other synthesizer products. Between 1973 and 1977, the company developed dozens of new keyboards carrying the Korg brand name. 1975 saw the introduction of the Maxi-Korg and the 900 PS polyphonic preset synthesizer. A year later, the PE-1000 (Polyphonic Ensemble) and PE-2000 (Polyphonic Ensemble Orchestra) were unveiled. The PS-3300 followed in 1977, and then came the MS10 and MS20 in 1978, which are still coveted by artists in the dance and techno genres."

[by Mark Vail, Keyboard, August 1996.
Additional text by Greg Rule and Korg Online www.korgusa.com.]

nine inch nails
mastermind
trent reznor

Extremist . . . Genius

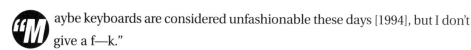

"Maybe keyboards are considered unfashionable these days [1994], but I don't give a f—k."

Trent Reznor isn't one to mince words. Since bursting onto the scene in 1989 with his Nine Inch Nails platinum debut *Pretty Hate Machine*, he's shocked, offended, and, amazed us with his twisted brilliance. In his hands, vintage synths, guitars, and raw samples become harsh, yet ingeniously crafted, electro-metal landscapes. Once-recognizable instruments are digitally stomped, scratched, and mangled into noisy byproducts using Digidesign Turbosynth and other, more fiendish, sample-editing techniques — ultimately to be layered with Reznor's own tortured voice. Even though he makes no bones about his hi-tech allegiance, Trent Reznor has surged to the forefront in a technology-hating genre.

Nine Inch Nails, circa 1997. Trent Reznor is pictured center, with programming prodigies Charlie Clouser and Chris Vrenna to his right, respectively.
◄ ·····························

"I think keyboards have been given a bad rap in rock music," he says with disgust. "The Pearl Jams and whoever, that's not what I'm about. I like keyboards. I like technology. This is who I am."

In mid-1992, after a real estate deal in New Orleans fell through, Reznor flew to L.A. in hopes of finding the ultimate home studio site. And boy did he ever . . . the infamous "Charles Manson" Tate mansion. Considering his affinity for things abnormal, the match wasn't too surprising. What was surprising was the fact that he picked the place unknowingly.

"On a whim, I came out to Los Angeles," he says, sprawled across a sofa at the Record Plant in Hollywood. "It was a whirlwind tour. I looked at maybe 15 houses in one day, and at that time I had no idea one of them was the Tate house. No one brought that to my attention, even though they should have."

After closing the deal, and driving halfway across the U.S. from his digs in New Orleans, Reznor wasted little time in transforming the spooky confines into a high-tech showcase. Rooms that once witnessed the deeds of Sir Charles were now home to a new breed of dementia. *The Downward Spiral* (Interscope), the result of his Tate tenure, is aggressive, rude, inventive, and unpredictable. The lyrics are cold, and packed with references to such items as pain, sex, and disease. From the opening cut, "Mr. Self Destruct," a jagged aural assault reminiscent of "Wish," to "Closer," an electro-groove laden with 808 drums and watery bass lines, Reznor's vision is distorted, unnerving, and altogether brilliant.

"This was a difficult record to make," he grimaces. "I didn't have a definite idea of how it should sound. I mean, I had a theme lyrically and vibe-wise, but musically I wanted to put more emphasis into textures and mood, and not rely on the same bag of tricks. I had to develop a whole new palette of sounds to work with.

"Another thing that delayed this record was me learning how to write again," he continues, "deciding what I wanted to do. I didn't want to make another *Broken* [Interscope]. I didn't want to box Nine Inch Nails into: 'Make every song harder than the last one, meaner, tougher.' I think that's a trap. That's not really what Nine Inch Nails is about. And I didn't want to go completely back to the *Pretty Hate Machine* style: percolating synth stuff. But I realized that when I sat

About the name Nine Inch Nails, Trent says, "It's just a name. Everyone's got a theory on that — nailing Jesus to the cross, or this and that. But it just came up. I like it. I like the way it looked in print, and it passed the two-week test."

down and started noodling around with ideas, I was much more inspired to sit at a keyboard than I was with a guitar."

A closet noodler Reznor isn't; he was classically trained on piano as a kid. And even though he doesn't like tooting his own horn, his studio chops aren't too shabby either. As a teen, he logged time as an employee of a Cleveland, Ohio, recording facility, an association that ultimately lead to the formation of Nine Inch Nails. Those unfamiliar with Reznor's past work might want to check out his hellish electronic stylings on *Pretty Hate Machine* and its six-song follow-up, *Broken*.

"With *Broken*," he explains, "I wanted to do something a lot harder than I did on *Pretty Hate Machine*. I wanted it to be a blast of destruction." *Broken* was made in secret because, according to Reznor, "we were in the midst of a legal tangle with TVT, our old record label."

At the time of this writing, Reznor was all too ready to kiss the studio world goodbye and get back to the altered reality of life on the road. I spent a day with Reznor at the Record Plant and learned firsthand about the aches, pains, bumps, and bruises associated with a do-it-yourself record.

Why did you decide to make this record at home?

I wanted to fine-tune my engineering skills; that's one thing we've always lacked in the Nine Inch Nails inner circle. I figured if I had a studio around, I'd inevitably figure out how to do it. And also, for the first time, we had the resources to do something right, so we ended up buying a big console and a couple of Studer machines because it was cheaper than renting, in the long run.

The project took considerably longer than anticipated. What happened?

We moved out here [to L.A.] on July 4, 1992. What we thought would take X amount of time to get a studio set up, ended up taking three times as long. As much as I enjoy equipment, fucking around with stuff, systems, and all that, there came a point where the whole focus was just to get the thing working and then learn it. Eventually I realized, "Okay, I'm sick of being in this room, now it's time to write an album." So I started writing, and by Christmas I had about four songs that I thought were decent.

Were there many gear snafus or other problems associated with working at home?

There were a couple pieces of gear crucial to the way the studio worked up at the house. One of them was a [Timeline] Micro-Lynx synchronizer. It syncs the two Studers, [Digidesign] Pro Tools, and everything. To be honest, it didn't work. Ten times a day we'd have to turn it off, unplug every cable, plug 'em back in, turn it back on, call the company, and, "Guess what? It doesn't work." There were many times when I thought, "Am I the only person in the world who's ever tried to hook these two pieces of gear, that they say work together, together?" So between that, and the terrible automation on the Amek board that we had, things would grind to a halt. I cannot tolerate equipment fucking up when you're trying to write a song, when you're on a roll. When you're in a [commercial] studio and something breaks, someone is usually there to fix it. When you're in a house, you're lying on your back under the board, scratching your head, trying to figure what the fuck. I mean, we can get people, but it might mean five hours of waiting around.

One danger when having a full studio in your house is: What do you focus on? I could spend, and have spent, a month just sampling things. So now, when it comes time to pull up a drum bank, it's all cool sounds that I've created, rather than leftovers from things I've used before. We spent a lot of time sampling and processing the sounds through different things. That way, when the actual writing and arranging moment came . . . when you went to reach for that bank of sounds, they were inspiring, instead of, "Fuck, I'm in the middle of writing a song, but I should really spend a couple of days getting all new Oberheim sounds."

What were some of the things you sampled?

My assistant, Chris Vrenna, probably went through 3,000 movies, listening to them without watching them. Not to find the cliché spoken dialog sample, but just to hear sounds. He'd throw them on DAT, then I'd listen to them — I didn't know where they came from — and I'd cut 'em up into little segments and process them further through Turbosynth or whatever. We compiled almost ten optical discs of "things" like that. We'd do a new song: "Okay, what's the mood?" "It's grim." So we'd put up a bank, find a sound, and set it aside.

Another thing I did was . . . a guy came to tune our studio, and he had one of those real-time frequency/noise-generator things. So I sampled it. I think there's something strangely musical about noise. If you take a high frequency, and pitch it way down to where it's aliasing, you've got a pretty cool thing. You layer that into the mix and it suddenly becomes thicker, even though sometimes you can't necessarily hear it. A song like "Mr. Self Destruct," obviously you're going to hear it; it sounds like a vacuum cleaner running through the whole thing. But a lot of times it just thickens things up without being noticed as, "Oh, he's layering some noise in there."

Let's get into the components of the record. Your drum tracks sound like a mixture of machines, samples, and maybe a bit of live drumming.

"My idea of a drum is a button on a drum machine."

Everything was programmed. My idea of a drum is a button on a drum machine. When I hear a real drum kit . . . when someone hits a kick drum, it doesn't sound to me like what I think a kick drum is. Any time I've been faced with, "Let's try miking up the drums," well, you put a mike up close, you put another one here, 300 mikes, gates, bullshit, overheads, bring 'em up and listen to it and it doesn't sound at all like it did in the room. It sounds like a "record-sounding drum kit." It doesn't sound like being in the room with live ringy drums. You read these interviews where producers will say, "It sounds like you're in the room with the band." No it doesn't. Nirvana's record doesn't sound like you're in the room with them. It might sound sloppy, and it sounds interesting, but it's not what it sounds like in the room, to me, anyway.

So we were experimenting with just two mikes, PZMs usually. We ended up taking a drum kit into about 25 different rooms — from sneaking into live rooms at A&M Studios to bathrooms to living rooms to a garage, outdoors. We didn't close-mike anything, just put mikes in the same position about the same distance away from the drums, then hit each drum at several velocities and recorded them on a DAT machine. Then we sampled them all in stereo with velocity splitting on the Akai S1100s. I noticed that when you sat down and played those on a keyboard, they sounded exactly the way they did in the room: shitty, ringy, you know. When I programmed them, and even when they were perfectly quantized, they didn't sound like a drum machine. And that, in itself, lent a strange, unexpected vibe to the thing. So on a few songs, we used that. I purposely made the drum programming very rigid, so that maybe someone will listen to it and think, "Is that a machine? Nah, can't be. No machine sounds that shitty." I like the idea of hearing a record and thinking, "That's guitar, bass, and drums," and then upon further inspection, "Wait a second, that's not what it appears to be." So that was one thing we did. And then sometimes, it was cool to say, "Well, let's see what those drums would sound like in the bathroom." So we'd load a different disc and use it with the same sequence.

Did you use drum machines?

Well, we sampled a Roland TR-808, as you have to these days. I try to avoid using it, but there's something about that low end. It's hard to beat that great low 808 kick. Actually, for "Closer," we sampled the kick drum off of an old Iggy Pop record, "Nightclubbing," off *Idiot*. Most everything was sampled, but I did use a Roland R-70, just because I wanted something that was a drum machine. I ended up being pretty impressed with its sounds, although they're somewhat generic-sounding. Good idea but terrible operating system.

Toward the end of the song "Piggy," it sounds very much like live drumming.

Okay, I confess, that one thing was live. For that part, I had a rigid, weird sixteenth-note pattern going. A kit was set up in the dining room, and I was play-ing along, fuckin' around, testing out the drums. I'd go in the other room, start the machine, run back in, put the headphones on, and play along. I couldn't hear it very good and I was way out of meter. So I just played as insanely as I could so I could hear how the drums were going to sound on tape. When I listened back, I thought, "Hey, that's pretty cool. Someday I'll come back and fix it." And of course I never did. That was it. That was the final take. A lot of what I do is accidental. I luck into things. I think that due to laziness — not coming back and fixing things — they end up becoming more interesting. My instinct is to repair, edit. "I'll get to it later." But then I'll get so used to hearing it, I'll end up leav-ing it alone.

How much of this album was recorded to hard disk?

Pretty much any real instrument like guitar or vocals or bass was recorded into the computer first; I use Opcode's Studio Vision all the time now for sequencing. Usually I'd loop something and then play along with it for awhile, then I'd go back and listen. If anything was decent, I'd cut it together into something cool. All the guitars I played were cut up and put together like that.

Did you mike the guitar cabinets or go direct?

I never mike cabinets. I've tried it, but I just don't like the sound that much — versus just going direct or through amp simulators. *Broken*, for example, had a lot of that super-thick chunk sound. Almost every guitar sound on that record was me playing through an old Zoom pedal, direct, and then going into

Turbosynth. Then I used a couple of key ingredients to make it sound unlike any real sound in the world, and layered about four of them together. By then, it wasn't a guitar anymore. It's an awesome sound.

The great thing about the guitar as an instrument is its expression. It's much more expressive than playing a keyboard. Unquestionably, the controller/input device of the strings is a lot more expressive and accidental and uncontrollable. When you then can take that, and process it in a computer environment, you still get some of those elements of randomness.

What are those "key ingredients" in Turbosynth you mentioned a minute ago?

Usually I call up the Waveshaper and click through a few of them, or Convert Sample to Oscillator sometimes. A real low pitch can get you some insane sounds. I also use the modulator: Taking the sound as one input, getting the oscillator module, taking something with a real low frequency that has a bell tone or some odd harmonics, and modulating those two can usually produce some awesome death vocal or guitar sounds.

Also, for guitar, almost everything was put through a Zoom 9030. I don't like the distortion stuff in there — it's too traditional-sounding — but I really like the amp simulator. We also have the new Marshall rackmount head, the JMP-1, I think it is. It's a great-sounding head. So I take the direct out of that through the amp simulator in the Zoom, and you can get a pretty good, almost Pantera-ish power-metal sound. I use that as a basis to start with, and since everything's recorded in the computer, it's easy to take it into Turbosynth and fuck around with it. Sometimes in real time, too. With [Digidesign] Sound Tools, I'll mess around in the parametric EQ window in real time when it's previewing. It's also outputting digital at that time, so I'll hook a DAT up and record it while it's previewing, sweep through stuff, and get some insane distortion stuff. Load that back into Studio Vision and you have a performance of an EQ thing that you couldn't do otherwise. We do a lot of stuff like that.

For "Mr. Self Destruct," we ran the whole mix through some old Neve mike pre's: a couple of channels of an old board. Those have great distortion; they're what I use for vocal distortion on almost everything. Those and the Zoom, which has a great ring modulator. I will say, though, that vocal distortion has

◄··································

**Stand and deliver.
Trent onstage
during the
*Downward
Spiral* tour.**

become an incredibly cliché thing these days. It's become overused and unin-
teresting. But I think there are varying degrees of blending it in, or different effects that can come across. I want people to hear what I'm saying, but then
again, I'm not interested in the great Phil Collins vocal sound. Maybe it's because
I'm insecure about my own vocals. I don't know. But it's my record, and I'm
gonna make it sound shitty if I want to.

What are the roles of your various synths and samplers?

Most everything is Akai samplers. I think the best thing about having some amount of success is the ability to get cool gear . . . not being bummed when some new sampler comes out that you know you can't afford. So we have two S1100s, each one with an expander, so essentially four samplers. And that works out perfectly: One's almost always used for drums, one for miscellaneous stuff, and so forth, with quite a bit of memory in each. Then it comes down to . . . I use the Minimoog a lot. I don't really like getting new synthesizers. It seems the emphasis now is building these all-in-one workstation same-sound ROM-playback bullshit things. I really kind of fell out of touch with what was happening until someone suggested I check out a Kurzweil K2000, which I did, and bought. I think that's the only keyboard I've bought recently that's new, that I think is potentially awesome. I don't know all I should know about it, but we used that a lot because of the fact that it can read Akai banks. To me, that's kind of like real-time Turbosynth that's MIDI-controllable in a sampling situation. So we'll take a drum bank from the Akai, load it into the Kurzweil, and set up the programmable sliders on my MIDI controller to control some parameter that modulates something. On the song "The Becoming," all the drums were done with the Kurzweil like that. You could never do that in the Akai. I was also surprised at the amount of shit that's in there. In the day of preset piano sounds, it's incredible that someone put that much thought into an instrument.

The bass sound on "The Becoming" was impressive.

That was the "Ober-Moog," or whatever it was going to be called [Oberheim OBMX]. I got it from Richard Bugg, my repair guy out here, who was one of the guys designing it. I asked him, "Have you heard about this Oberheim-Moog thing?" And he says, "Yeah, I've got one out at the house. Wanna borrow it for a while?" "Bring it on over!" That thing is the fuckin' greatest-sounding keyboard in the world, because it sounds like a Minimoog and an Oberheim, and you can run each one through each other. It doesn't quite work right, and unfortunately the project was scrapped, but that's what I used. It shows up in a couple of places mainly because I was getting bored using the Minimoog, which I've used for almost every bass sound I've ever done. So now I use the Minimoog a lot more for running stuff through its external input and through the filter. Aside from that, I still use the Oberheim Xpander, but it's role has decreased a little bit; I'm just kind of bored with it. And the Prophet-VS, I still use that.

I have a PPG, and I have a Waldorf MicroWave. If I go about trying to program that thing in a logical way, it comes out sounding like mid-1980s synth-pop — kind of dated, digital-sounding. But just through randomly generating stuff with Opcode's Galaxy, and I did this a lot on the Xpander and the VS, I'd generate thousands and thousands of programs. Then I'd hear an element of one that was cool, and fine-tune it. That may be a cop-out way of programming, but it was pretty interesting to find out, "What did it do to make it sound like that?" Then you go in and look and see what it did randomly. Every patch I have in the Waldorf is from that origin.

You mentioned having difficulty with your synchronizer. Did you have any similar problems keeping your synths, samplers, and hard disk tracks in line?

Not too much, really. Studio Vision was great — very few hassles keeping stuff together, in that respect. But we're not too anal about . . . if something is happening, we'll try to work around it. We'll figure out how to fix it later. We do a lot of stuff really sloppy on certain levels. On other levels, it's a very laboratory-like environment.

But problems? Sometimes I'd be in the studio and discover, "Why are all the vocals I've recorded suddenly in the wrong pitch and out of sync?" Then you realize that tape calibration somehow got turned on in Studio Vision — some mysterious element that changed the pitch and the tempo of the sequence and . . . it's gone, you'll never get it back at that point. You can diddle around with equations, pitch-shift everything down, slow it down X amount. Forget it. Go have a beer, come back the next day, and start over.

What was it like working with Flood?

Flood is an awesome guy, the best programmer I've ever been around in my life. You tend to work a certain way, which is very methodical — chisel away. "The completion of your record is so far away, don't even think about it. Just think about the completion of this hi-hat program." Then I read where Nirvana recorded and mixed an album in two weeks, and I'm going, "Fuck, that's gonna sell a lot more than mine is." There's got to be some balancing. So the next record I'm gonna do is going to be one that's a lot more spontaneous. One that better hides the horrors of technology, which can bog you down to a crawl. Many a time I've been sitting in front of an Akai with its ridiculous, archaic operating system, trying to put these 400 samples into this keygroup and . . . "Why am I doing this? This is stupid. Why haven't I hired someone to do this for me yet?" That's another thing that led to the delay in putting out this record: getting bogged down in the studio. "There are 40 things I could do right now. I could write a song, which is the most important, or I could sample drums, or I could try EQing this, or programming that," and so on. It's lacking the discipline and focus to say, "Forget all the fun stuff. I'm going to sit down and write a song."

In addition to the familiar NIN suspects, did you collaborate with any other outside artists?

We had [guitarist] Adrian Belew come in just to see what would happen. He showed up, and, "Hi, what do you want me to do?" And Flood and I were like, "Well, we don't know." So he looks at us, scratches his head, "All right, what key is it in?" We look at each other, "Hmm, not sure. Probably *E*. Here's the tape, do whatever you want to do. Go!" So he started noodling around and . . . Adrian is the most awesome musician in the world. I've never seen anybody play guitar like that.

How are you going to pull this music off live?

Well, the thing I learned from the last tour . . . the dilemma that I faced was: I didn't want to have three guys onstage, faking everything, with a tape machine running. However, I also didn't want a seven-piece rock band where every cool bit of electronic-ness was converted into people approximating it live on other instruments. I don't use electronics as a cop-out: "I couldn't get a drummer, so I just programmed it," or, "I couldn't play this part good enough, so I programmed it." It's not that kind of thing at all. I program because I like the way it sounds. I like quantization. I enjoy the sound of it. I like using those elements of perfection amidst randomness. And live, I didn't want that element to be brushed under the table by a big live band. So we used four tracks of tape and four musicians: I'd play guitar on some songs, and sing, plus a keyboard player, a guitar player, and a drummer.

At the time there were no digital four-track devices that were affordable to us, so we just used a four-track cassette deck — high-speed Tascam special. One track would be a click that the drummer would play to; he'd wear headphones onstage. One track would be bass, because 90 percent of the bass was synth, and I wouldn't want a real guy playing a bass, simulating that, nor would I want to see a keyboard player tapping sixteenth-notes out with his head down. And the other two tracks were stereo miscellaneous. Maybe it would be a percussion loop. Maybe it would be some sequency-sounding keyboard part. Stuff like that. And all the drums, vocals, main keyboard parts, and guitars were being played live.

I don't feel like I have to justify why we used tape onstage — I've always admitted that, and I will admit that we're going to do it again on the next tour — but the point was, that was the best way to get the stuff across live. That was the best way to maintain what was good about the electronic side of it. I didn't want to take sequencers and shit out live: "Excuse me, ladies and gentlemen, while I get on my back and get under the keyboard rig and figure out what MIDI cable isn't plugged in." I mean, we had enough problems with the one piece of gear that can fuck us up: the tape deck. We had a lot of problems with that. The only MIDI onstage was from triggers on the drum kit. The keyboard player just had an [E-mu] Emax; he'd load a disk for each song.

Did you ever feel inhibited, improvisation-wise, by using tapes?

Obviously you can't extend the end of a song, but I've never done that anyway, so I don't miss it.

What will the lineup be for this tour?

Since we never played most of the *Broken* stuff out live — which is way heavier on guitar, and I don't want to be bogged down playing complicated guitar parts and singing — I've got Chris Vrenna on drums, James Wooley on keyboards, and two new guys, Danny Lohner and Robin Finck, each of whom is a guitar player/keyboard player/bass player. They're the best musicians I've had involved in the band so far. I even foresee moments when everybody is playing keyboards onstage.

Are you planning to take an ADAT, DA-88, or whatever, on tour this time?

Yeah. That's the plan right now. We're testing both kinds to see which one is more roadworthy. But essentially, my band can play more now, so the decision to move to eight tracks is based purely on the fact those machines are digital and available, and not because we necessarily need more tracks. I mean, we are going to experiment with some things like putting timecode on it, and we're orchestrating a production where some cues could be timecode-based to some lighting stuff. Not a totally automated light show, but there could be things . . . this is all hypothetical, but we're talking about some back speakers for surround things where a couple of tracks on the tape could be used for certain effects. One thing is certain: I'll never go back out with a Tascam cassette deck which has the irritating problem of stopping whenever there's a voltage spike or anything. That has led to a few problems with us onstage.

Care to expound upon any of those hellish gig experiences?

Opening day, Lollapalooza, Phoenix. We couldn't play because one of the power boxes had melted, and every time the low end of the P.A. would rumble, it would jiggle the cord and all power onstage would just shut off and turn back on. If you have a sampler, that means you're down for a minute. And if you have a tape deck, ahem, that means it stops. But I think because we were an "electronic" band, everyone was just waiting for us to fuck up onstage. So this started happening and: "Hello, does anybody know what's going on?" A voice from backstage: "No, but I think it's working now." Turn to the crowd: "Okay, hey, we suck, so here's our next song." And ten seconds into it, every time he hit the kick drum, there it went. Turn back around: "This is the biggest show we've ever played, does anyone know what the fuck is wrong?" Voice from backstage: "We think we have it!" Turn to the crowd: "Okay, one more time," and . . .

So what did you do?

We smashed all the gear and ran to the bus.

*[by Greg Rule, **Keyboard**, **March 1994**]*

A year and a half later, I met up with Trent again. He had declined nearly all media requests at the time, but he graciously cleared his schedule for this interview. When the okay came in, I caught the first flight to Hartford, Connecticut, where the Nails were just days away from kicking off a major dual tour with David Bowie (slated to feature a nightly set where Bowie teams with Trent to play Nine Inch Nails music and vice-versa). In a gutted hotel room turned makeshift production studio, Trent cued up to the tape recorder.

Unlike the man we've all become accustomed to on video and stage, he was in a kind, gentle frame of mind. He was polite, thoughtful, and no, he didn't smash or set fire to any of his gear that day. "Contrary to popular belief, I'm not a vampire," he said, smiling. "My reflection does show up in a mirror." Don't get the wrong idea, though. Trent was still Trent; he was booked into the hotel under the pseudonym Dr. Hannibal Lector.

Trent's traveling rig was a technologist's dream — and a hotel maid's nightmare. "We don't let the maids in," joked drummer Chris Vrenna, pointing to day-old food leftovers and piles of trash as proof. Cables, racks, and instruments were strewn from end to end. Anvil cases were stacked chin-high in the bathroom. Components of the confines included a Macintosh Quadra 950 with a 10GB drive running Opcode's Studio Vision a channels), and, in alphabetical order, an Akai S1100, Clavia Nord Lead, E-mu EIV, FocusRite compressor and EQ, Korg Wavedrum, Kurzweil K2000, Mackie 32-channel 8-Bus and LM-3204 mixers, Oberheim Xpander, Peavey Spectrum Analog Filter, Roland Super Jupiter, R-70 drum machine, vintage Roland Vocoder, Sequential Prophet-VS, Tascam DA-88, Waldorf MicroWave, Yamaha VL-1m, and Zoom 9050 effects processor.

As before, Trent unleashed mouthfuls of quotable material in this interview. This time, however, the focus was on the state of technology, censorship, his studio setup in New Orleans, and his future projects (including a possible venture into the music software business).

Now . . . where did we put that garlic necklace Trent gave us?

Last time we talked, you were just getting ready to hit the road. Here we are a year and a half later, and you're still on tour. How have you and the band been holding up?

Pretty good. There was a time, right around February of this year, when it had gone on too long without a break. It got redundant playing the same set night after night, and there was a phase where I really just didn't want to tour anymore. Then they came up with, "Do you want to go to Australia for three or four shows and some festivals?" "Hmm, this might be kind of fun. We'll try it." And halfway through the first set the first night it was like being right back on that last week. It wasn't good. So I got busy setting up a studio in New Orleans, kind of getting a home base there.

A permanent installation?

Yeah. We bought a 48-track analog studio, and the concept at that early time was to get out of a real studio to do stuff in a different environment. A big lesson I learned from the Tate house experience is not to live where your studio is, because it just became an entrapment. There's also a million distractions that will keep you from working — kind of the opposite of what I originally thought. That record [*The Downward Spiral*] probably took longer because you're working and the phone rings, and it's UPS at the gate with a delivery. All those kind of things happen because it's your house. So when I decided to go live in New Orleans again, I casually looked around for a temporary space to set up shop, and we found this place. It was perfect. It was real big, cheap, and that idea mutated into a more permanent installation, maybe because there aren't any studios in New Orleans that are right for what I do. What it's going to end up being is a pretty cool SSL room, an analog 48-track place, that sounds really good. It just got functional right when we left to go on tour.

What are your feelings about trusting outsiders in the studio?

I do to a degree. I think my collaborative efforts with Flood and Alan Moulder worked. I've learned that you need some outside objectivity at times. There's other times. . . . I mean, when I produce Marilyn Manson and Prick, I think I have that objectivity that the artist doesn't have. They're hearing that lyric being funny or they're hearing that one note out of tune, and they might be missing the big picture that this is a statement. Like on the Prick album, Kevin and I worked on four of those tracks in my bedroom when I was doing *Broken*. It was a situation where we'd talked about working together, we'd been friends for a long time, and I'd always respected his stuff. He sent me a tape of some stuff that sounded so ridiculous; it was great. It sounded like someone who didn't know how to work a drum

> **"I listen to what's popular now in rock music, and the idea of a guitar, bass, and drum band in the Nirvana mold is just so utterly boring to me. Not that there aren't good songs that come out of that, or good bands — Nirvana being one of them — but to me, to get a band together that just, 'Okay, G, D . . .' It's been done. It's been done to death. If you're going to make music, have something to say, and have some unique way to say it."**

machine. But I'd never heard anything like it because he couldn't do that if he knew how to. . . . A bad thing about getting some good engineers is that you can't get them to do things wrong. "That's not how you do that." "Well, try." But it had that kind of creative element to it. We sat and messed around with a Yamaha TX802, four tracks of Pro Tools running Studio Vision, a couple of keyboards, and a DAT machine, and it became a challenge of, "How can we arrange this music with these limitations?" It was one mike in a room, and if there were background vocals it was me yelling from the other side of the room, and mixing everything destructively — mix these down to two tracks and keep going — and we ended up with four songs. So four years later, ironically enough, signed to my label, he worked with other producers. And when we were assembling the record, just for the fuck of it, I put the old mixes up and, technically, they weren't mixed good, but there was some sort of energy spark there that was way better than the other ones that took days trying to recreate the accidents that occurred there.

Accidents?

Studio Vision at that time couldn't play back as many cuts as I had in this one part through the [Digidesign] DAE, so it for some reason would put this thing

"To fall into that trap of, 'To have it be real music it's gotta be real instruments or real people playing it' is complete nonsense."

up an octave and skip through another section, and it became a hook that if it wasn't in there the song didn't sound right. So on the album we ended up using the original mixes. I was trying to explain to Kevin that when those elements of magic occur, take advantage of it. Bob Clearmountain might be pissed off when he hears that album, but nobody else cares.

Chris Vrenna said Bob Clearmountain was screaming for aspirin after he mixed you at Woodstock.

[*Laughs.*] That was our thing in the studio: "Would Bob Clearmountain hate it?" "Yeah." "It's good then." [*Laughs.*]

Chris also said you were toying with the idea of possibly recording Nine Inch Nails live in the studio. What's your vision of the next NIN record?

Well, it fluctuates. I'd say it'll probably end up being a hybrid, because my latest thing I'm hot to do is collaborate with some other people. Probably at the top of my list this second is Mike Garson from Bowie's band. He's a phenomenal pianist/keyboardist. We've been messing around at the soundchecks, just playing stuff, and I don't understand how that sound's coming out of his instrument. He's coming from a place that's far removed from me, but kind of how I used Adrian Belew [guitarist] on the last record, I'd love to feed him some of the things like that. I'd like to work with different groups of people for different ideas. The idea of live is intriguing because I've done every record pretty much based on the same format of programming. I like the idea of doing a record that is performed and then treated maybe in an Eno fashion. I listen to what's popular now in rock music, and the idea of a guitar, bass, and drum band in the Nirvana mold of music is just so utterly boring to me. Not that there aren't good songs that come out of that, or good bands — Nirvana being one of them — but to me, to get a band together that just, "Okay, *G*, *D* . . ." It's been done. It's been done to death. If you're going to make music, have something to say, and have some unique way to say it. To me, I look at the studio as a tool, an instrument. There's so much you can do sonically. To fall into that trap of, "To have it be real music it's gotta be real instruments or real people playing it" is complete nonsense. I like the challenge of doing a record, maybe Nine Inch Nails, maybe not, of a traditional instrumentation but seeing how far out you could get without sounding like Nirvana.

People might wonder if there might ever come a time when we see you on TV, smiling gleefully, singing about a mountain stream or whatever.

That's a hard one to answer, but if I felt that way, that's what my music would be like. Yeah. If I went through such a sudden change, though, I think Nine Inch Nails would gracefully bow out as an entity and I would become whatever else.

What's the story behind the name Nine Inch Nails?

It just was a name. Everyone's got their theory on that — nailing Jesus to the cross, or this and that. But it just came up. I liked it. I liked the way it looked in print, and it passed the two-week test.

How do you think Nine Inch Nails would sound unplugged?

[*Grins.*] I had a few theories on that. My favorite one was us onstage with our equipment, and I'd look at Chris and say, "Start the tape." He reaches over and pushes play, and of course it's not on, it's unplugged. You can see the plug hangin' there. And I say, "Start the tape, Chris," and he pushes the start button and, nothing. So we just smash our instruments and leave. [*Laughs.*] But I've thought about interesting ways to . . . the thought I've had is . . . I've hung with Rick Rubin [producer] a lot, who's most likely going to produce a new Nine Inch Nails album, because I think it's an anti-Flood-type mentality, which I think is good because I need to have a new change. And I know he's much more traditional song-oriented. I've looked at most of my music and it's based on a groove or a mood, and I make a song around that versus a song that's based on traditional harmonic chord progressions or whatever. So as a writer I've been thinking more in terms of seeing what it would be like to go in that direction a bit. And I don't mean becoming more conventional, but maybe starting with a song and then arranging it in any fashion. Just little games you play to trick yourself into things. At the same time, I also like the idea of removing those elements and see-ing how far removed from a traditional song you can get and still have an ele-ment of something catchy about it.

Charlie Clouser [Nine Inch Nails keyboardist] programmed a batch of tracks for White Zombie's *Astro Creep 2000* — songs that often have only one or two chords that cycle through the whole thing.

But there are choruses hidden in there, and that's the thing. You can have one note go through the whole song, but when he [Rob Zombie, singer of White Zombie] starts singing "More human than human," that's the chant-along chorus. Most of Ministry's songs are one riff for as many bars as you can stand it, but it's still catchy because it does relate to something, as opposed to, say, some vintage Skinny Puppy where there is no element of . . . what you think might be a chorus never comes back, which I think can be either rambling nonsense or an interesting format. I'm into songs that are breaking out of that mold that I've fallen prey to: verse, chorus, verse, chorus, bridge, solo section, chorus, chorus. Almost every one of my songs fits that same structure. I heard a track by the band Shudder To Think, and I thought, "What in the fuck? The meter's weird. Nothing repeats until the very end where there's this little chant. It's fuckin' cool shit." So I went out and got the record. The structure of that was weird, but it worked. Another thing . . . Bowie was an influence during his *Low* period. That was a big influ-ence on *The Downward Spiral* from a point of, not only the mood and the des-peration that it had, but structurally the songs are bizarre. One might not have any vocals, but you don't even realize it. You didn't even miss it. Or there's an-other one: verse, chorus, fade out. Just things like that where they break up that tried-and-true formula. Or odd tempos. I liked Rush when I was a kid, and I still appreciate that, but it became a situation of playing odd tempos just because we could. I remember being in cover bands trying to play "Spirit of the Radio" and you couldn't count it, you were just memorizing the phrase. So I've tried to fuck around with odd meters, but trying to get it to flow. I like watching people who aren't musicians trying to bob their heads to "March of the Pigs," and they can't figure out why they keep getting off.

"Closer" was a big hit despite its hook line: "I want to f—k you like an animal." Did it bother you when you heard that song being played with the f-word bleeped out?

That song kind of came about . . . it just started with that line, and then the music built itself around that. That was the scariest song to write, because there would have been a time when I wouldn't have allowed myself to be that obvious, because I would have been afraid that it wasn't tough enough, or it was too disco. When I was writing it and I came up with that bass line, I thought, "This is so obvious, but fuck it." I mean, if you listen to the whole album, that song, musically, is the most digestible if you're trying to pick a single, but it's also crippled from the start because of the chorus. But I'm not going to change it to try to make it a single.

So do you think bleeping the f-word was the best solution?

On one hand, yes. I mean, I saw somebody's little kid singing it, a five-year-old kid. And I've got to question my own intentions in that department. But aside from that, what I've tried to make Nine Inch Nails about is to try to subversively sneak some things into. . . . I realize we have a pretty big audience now, so how can I take that position and slip some things in that are potentially dangerous ideas? Not to decay the moral fiber of America, but to have something of substance to think about other than just fluff. With all this controversy about some lyrics, I was surprised that we didn't get blasted sooner than we did. But their own idiocy and lack of knowledge crippled their argument. I would find lyrically a lot of the things on *The Downward Spiral* more dangerous than the comedic gangster rap stuff that no one takes seriously.

But when the song started to take off, it surprised me. What I hoped would have been a higher art thing became a frat house, date-rape, strip club anthem thing. Sad. I mean, it is an ugly song, no doubt. It's not nice. It's not life-affirmative. It's probably the ugliest on the record, which is why I dressed it up in nice easy-to-listen-to music. A nice juxtaposition to the lyrics. But as culture moves on and people become less inhibited by religious oppression and are encouraged to think for themselves — if people get over the silliness and the tools and mechanisms of organized religion that are used to invoke fear — things would be a lot better. It's something like the primitive stage the Internet's at now. Just to have information available to anybody anywhere that's non-governed and non-censored. You can find things now that your library doesn't have that's current and it's on every computer. It soon will be on every TV set. It's going to open people's minds up to more things. I think censorship has been causing a lot of problems in a lot of different departments in terms of human evolution. But, hey, that's what this country is based on — the ridiculous right wing, keep you in line, don't think too hard mentality.

Speaking of the Internet, what are your feelings about multimedia, be it CD-ROMs, enhanced CDs, Web sites, and the like — do you plan to dive in?

I've done quite a bit of thinking about that; we've had a couple of propositions from different CD-ROM-type multimedia people. So I did my degree of research of just checking out what's out there now, and I've had some conversations with Todd Rundgren, but, you know, as forward-thinking as I want to believe that I am right now, I approach that with a real degree of hesitation because I haven't seen any that I think are good yet. And I blame that on where the hardware is today. Everybody seems to bring commerce into it. To make it worth your while to produce it, it should run on a machine that's mainstream enough to warrant putting it out, which means the incredibly shitty Sega-CD systems or a PC. I don't think anybody wants to listen to music on a computer, or go through the hassle of having to have a couple thousand dollar computer just to do what? To see a flickery, shitty-looking video along with some lyrics? I haven't been impressed with the ones I've seen, although I haven't seen the EBN [Emergency Broadcast Network] one yet. I like the idea of it, but that also brings up another element of: Do people really want to interact with music, or do they just want to listen to it? The idea of an interactive movie where you actually control some degree of what's going on, that seems a bit closer to me than, here's a CD where you can remix some of the tracks and you can do this. Todd Rundgren's is an interesting one, but I can't imagine fucking with it for more than maybe a couple of hours. With a record, I can listen to it in a car, or I can put it on and it does the work for me.

The most interesting one we had presented to us was a demo by a company in England called ESP, and it was for the Phillips CD-I, which, again, is another failed platform. But you put this in, and it actually hacks into the operating system of the unit, so everytime you run it, it's different. What's really in there is several videos, and there is going to be an interactive interview with me where you could type in words, and I'd respond if it could recognize the text. And if you asked me irritating questions then I'd give shitty answers, and finally just leave. What they tried to do was put an element of chaos and personality into this disc, so maybe the joystick this time went in the opposite direction, or it would be difficult to control, or different buttons did random things. You didn't know what all was on there, so I thought it was an interesting way to add depth to something.

If it gets to the point where everybody's television set has a CD player hooked up to it, and they can put a CD in and see full-frame, full-motion video with no lag time, and good audio coming out of stereo speakers, anyone can get it, they're as common as CD players, then that will be the time to seriously consider the medium. When I pointed that out to Todd, he said, "Yeah, but someone has to be there in the interim. There are shortcomings, but someone has to do it." And I agree with that, but I have such a level of perfection to what I do that I'm not comfortable with it yet. Now, at the same time, I've always been fascinated with video games, and we are involved with the guys who made *Doom*, id Software. They're making a new one called *Quake* which is a *true* 3D world. Like all the other games, it's totally politically incorrect, gory and violent and scary. We met up with them, and I'm involved in the actual sounds for this environment — which is not music, it's textures and ambiences and whirling machine noises and stuff. We tried to make the most sinister, depressive, scary, frightening kind of thing. You'll be able to hook hundreds of people up together over the phone lines and see each other walking around, kill each other, *et cetera*. That's an interesting little side project that, I think, works really well with the technology that exists. It's been fun.

Are you going to launch an official Nine Inch Nails Web site?

We're working on a Web site for Nothing Records which will be primarily a database of information of all the bands, with lots of links. But there's a kid who's set one up out of Florida, and it's pretty impressive. We're just going to hire him to work for us — mutate his to be a real one. Part of the reason of commerce is that there will be merchandise available through there. That's the business reason to justify it, but my main reason is just as a source of information. Hopefully this will help us get rid of 98% percent of the false information that seems to be circulating about us.

Like, whether we can see your reflection in the mirror?

[*Laughs*] For starters.

There have been rumblings about you possibly getting involved in music software manufacturing. What's that all about?

Charlie [Clouser] and myself are talking about starting a software company to put out some very specialized DSP-type software, maybe in the form of plug-ins, but more likely mini-stand-alone applications like SoundHack. Little things. Ways to fuck up, degrade, and mutate sounds that aren't real commercial. Weird stuff. We found ways to destroy sounds, like taking the sample rate down to 2 bits, that you're not able to do in [Passport's] Alchemy or [Digidesign's] Sound Designer, and weird modulated things where you can really get shitty sounds. Maybe we'll incorporate, say, 30 of our favorite destructive processes — again, Bob Clearmountain would have no use for this [*laughs*]. Stuff like, "What if you took this and reduced its dynamic range down to zero?" Or, "What would happen if you took the sample rate down to this?" Whatever. We're collecting as many ideas as we can.

Have you set any solid goals or a time frame to realize this?

We're just talking about it right now — thinking about getting some people involved. No real time frame yet.

What do you think about the current crop of music technology?

Well, being a gear-head, I hadn't been interested in any new stuff that had come out, as far as keyboards, with the exception of the K2000. There was the hump of everything being workstations and sounding the same, the sample-playback shit just was not interesting. However with the modeling stuff — we picked up the Yamaha VL-1 after everyone said it was a piece of shit, and we borrowed it for an afternoon in New York, and I was probably the most blown away by it than with any keyboard I've met in years. I haven't delved into it far enough to know, "Oh, it can only do these three sounds," or not, but. . . . Like, I remember when I first heard a [Roland] D-50. It would have taken me five keyboards to make the sound, and that first moment it was, "Whoa!" And then you quickly realize that that's all it really can do. But the idea of organic sounds is right in line with a lot of things I've been fuckin' around with. I'm glad that somebody's put the research into a high-end piece of gear that's very noncommercial that has the ability to make some truly new-type sounds that are cool. I'm totally into that idea of technology. I also got the Roland guitar thing, the VG-8, and I think it's excellent for certain things. Just to be able to tune each string independently made it worthwhile. We were going to use it on tour but decided it probably wasn't a good idea, yet. But we used it on the new Marilyn Manson record, and I just think it's a cool idea, a cool concept. I think the clean sound is fantastic. If you look at it as an elaborate effects processor, I think it could succeed on that level.

And you have a Nord Lead.

I've got *four* of 'em now. I think that is the coolest-sounding analog-type synth. I just love it. And I think it looks cool, and that's pretty much the main reason I got it [*laughs*]. I love that keyboard, and I know it's going to make a lot of the [analog] shit I have now obsolete — like, it doesn't go out of tune.

What software do you prefer these days?

I tried other sequencers, but I keep going back to [Opcode] Vision. I couldn't be happier with it. [He also wrenches Digidesign's Pro Tools daily.]

Do you get much time to play keyboards away from the band?

I usually have the K2000 in my hotel room, but now that I have a place to put it, I'm going to get a piano. That was a nice thing about the Record Plant, they had a piano and I could just sit down and play alone.

Perhaps a solo piano album is in your future?

Yeah, in a couple years when no one likes me anymore.

You might be ideally suited to interpret, say, Cowell's "Banshee."

Yeah, but with hammers and nails and shit all over the thing. [*Laughs.*]

[by Greg Rule, Keyboard, December 1995]

ppg wave

german engineer Wolfgang Palm's line of PPG Wave instruments is without a doubt the most familiar line of vintage synthesizers to emerge from Germany. They're famous for their piercing digital sound, which brazenly included clock and aliasing noise in higher registers — musical grunge that gave the PPG that special sonic squawk. Perhaps the most popular PPG Wave sound was created by its ability to sweep through digital wavetables using envelope generators.

The span of Palm-developed electronic music products ranges from 1975 to the present. Although PPG is no longer in business, one of Palm's more recent developments can be found in the synthesis circuits of the Waldorf MicroWave — the '90s-vintage PPG Wave instrument.

As with most synth pioneers, Palm's quest began small, and slowly snowballed. "In the early '70s, I was playing organ in a small band in Hamburg," he recalls. "Nobody in Germany had a synthesizer at

vital stats

Description: The first widely available digital wavetable synthesizer, with analog filters, sequencing, and user sampling option.

Production Dates: Wave 2.2, 1982-84; Wave 2.3, 1984-87.

Manufacturer: PPG (Palm Products Germany), Wandsbecker Zollstraße 89, 2000 Hamburg Wandsbeck, West Germany (out of business).

Approximate Number Made: Wave 2.2, 300; Wave 2.3, 700.

Original Prices: PPG Wave 2.2, $8,800; PPG Wave 2.3, $9,000-$10,000 (later discounted to about $6,500).

that time. So I built my own VCOs and connected them to my organ keyboard. I made some crazy things, including simple sequencers. Then I built some special keyboards for the guy who handled Moog's distribution in Germany. That led to my association with the members of Tangerine Dream, particularly Chris Franke and Edgar Froese. They had a great interest in new instruments, so they invested a lot of money and time and ideas, and helped me start my business."

Within a few years, Palm designed what he calls "the first programmable synthesizer," the PPG 1003. "It was a very strange instrument, with no knobs on the front panel, only increment and decrement buttons. All my customers were very afraid of it, because they didn't know how to handle it. I think we sold only six pieces of that machine."

But it was a start. His next goal — around 1977, when Oberheim's monster, two-case Eight Voice was the rage — was to produce a cheap polyphonic synthesizer that made new sounds. Palm's idea was to replace the VCOs, VCFs, and VCAs with digital oscillators for harmonic control and tuning stability. He hoped that wavetable synthesis, in which waveforms are generated by a computer reading a set of numbers stored in memory, would suffice without the need of analog filtering. During his groundbreaking research, he found that the sound of simple waveforms produced digitally at 8-bit resolution wasn't as aesthetically appetizing as the fat mass of sound generated by the analog machines from his American competitors. At that time (1980/81), he was obliged to settle on 8-bit sound because of cost factors.

Palm knew he had to develop complex wavetables to improve the sound quality of his synths. But even with more complex waveforms, he eventually

In a time when analog synthesizers dominated the market, German engineer Wolfgang Palm chose a different direction with the digital PPG Wave.

realized that 8-bit digital sound was too brittle. "I found that wavetable switching wasn't smooth enough," he says, "So I returned to analog and connected a VCF and VCA to the digital oscillator. That was the Wave 2."

By 1982, Palm had advanced to the next generation, the Wave 2.2. Its configuration sounds remarkedly similar to some late-'80s synth/sequencer combos: eight-voice polyphony with two digital oscillators per voice, analog filtering, a pressure-sensitive keyboard, 200 patches, an eight-track digital sequencer, a ten-function arpeggiator, numerous split and layered keyboard modes, and an event generator that you used to control the sequencer. The 2.2's oscillators could generate almost 2,000 different single-cycle waveforms (some created from samples of acoustic instruments like sax and piano), a huge increase over anything else that was available at the time.

Meanwhile, Palm continued to develop his instrument's sample-playback capabilities. "In the Wave 2.2," he explains, "you could only play very small periods that consisted of 128 samples. The next step was the 2.3, in which the hardware was changed, and there were two modes. One was the digital oscillator mode, and the other was a sampler mode where you could play through the entire memory in a linear fashion, like on a sampler. Of course, you could transfer waveforms from one mode to the other, which was very interesting. You could sample something and then take out periods, make Fourier analyses, and put that back into a wavetable."

The Wave 2.3 was introduced at the 1984 Frankfurt Music Fair. Not only did it allow linear playback of samples in memory, but the resolution of those samples was increased to 12-bit, which improved the Wave's sound quality. The 2.3 was also multitimbral, and it had MIDI, the implementation of which is somewhat of a sore subject as far as Wolfgang Palm is concerned. "PPG had an 8-bit parallel buss system before MIDI came out," he says, "because we had to transfer samples from the Waveterm to the Wave — a very thick amount of data. Our buss was much quicker, so we didn't like MIDI very much. It was okay for some things. The problem was, MIDI was the second interface that we had to use and support. It took much more effort to redesign our existing machines than it would have been to implement all the MIDI capabilities from the beginning."

PPG synth sales started eroding in the mid-'80s, and like many American synth manufacturers, the company eventually called it quits, even though it had a good reputation among synthesists. Wolfgang Palm summarizes the difficulties: "The PPG keyboards didn't sell so well anymore because everybody came out with a sampler. The truth is, I was never a real businessman; I'm just a developer. In the end, running the PPG business was a lot of hassle and stress; it was not the thing I really wanted. It was the thing that had to be done because, of course, you must earn money and you must sell machines."

[by Mark Vail, Keyboard, January 1992]

björk and mark bell

Writing, Recording, and Performing *Homogenic*

*i*celandic folklore is as strange as trolls, fearful as the devil, and happy as the peasant girl rewarded half the kingdom for finding the lost prince. These kinds of stories haven't gone unnoticed by Björk; as a teenager, she self-published 100 copies of her own fairy tale, "Um Urnot." Still in tune with eerie Nordic tales about what lurks in the night, she describes the embryos of her songs as "green hairy lumps."

Her third solo Elektra album, *Homogenic* — recorded in southern Spain — sits darkly "at the bottom of the ocean." But Björk asserts that "it's got lots and lots of hope," and the songs suggest they're on the verge of floating up to oxygen and light. The curtain rises on "Hunter," with military snare rolls panned hard right, the waxing rush of an Icelandic string octet, long inhales of reversed accordion, and Björk's emotive cry, "I thought I could organize freedom. How Scandinavian of me!" She's the Pippi Longstocking of popular music, seemingly girlish and yet outrageously independent. A leg ahead of the pop mainstream, she shapes music that stabs us in the jugular, even though our first reaction might have been: "Huh? Those beats just sound like a bunch of farts."

Known globally for her cutting-edge solo records, Björk first gained fame as a member of the Sugar Cubes in the late '80s.

Ask her to talk about bpms, new machines, and writing music, and Björk will conjure up enough analogies to drown an entire desert in a mirage pond. She crinkles her brow and shakes a disapproving forefinger at synths mimicking flutes and violins, likening the faux sounds to white-trash lawn furniture. Ironically, the Reykjavik-born 32-year-old minimizes her own intelligence without hesitation. About the album title she admits, "I think the word doesn't exist, but I'm so stupid that I thought it meant 'homogenous.' By the time somebody told me it was actually bullshit, I thought, 'Okay then. I'll stay with it.'"

Björk commands the full breadth of her voice over cartoon beats and a glass harmonica. She makes no apologies for eccentric sounds, knowing that trying to please everybody could leave them all miserable. After a 20-year career, she's still looking through a microscope at her artistic insides: "I think after all those years, I've slowly gotten closer to what I'm about, but I've still got a long way to go. . . ."

analogy-sorceress

To Björk, beats are much more than a means to practice aikido moves on a dance floor, or even for keeping the momentum going in a melody. She sees a direct correlation between the rhythm of our hearts (a word she says with such fervor, it's as if she's growling and gargling at the same time) and the rhythm of our songs. "It's completely linked," she says. "Beats per minute or rhythms are completely linked with the heartbeat and how much blood is pumped into our body. 120 beats per minute is happy, we are humans being happy and you get happy house. 160 bpm, which is drum 'n' bass, is generally thought of as angry. And when we are very angry, our heart goes up to 160. When we are calm, we want chill-out music or ambient; our heart goes down to 70, even 60. In a way, beats represent the network of blood in our body, whereas something like a voice maybe represents the oxygen that travels around our body."

Björk takes a sudden detour from her beat philosophy to relay some not-so-common knowledge: "A lot of singers are very claustrophobic. They are so obsessed with oxygen that they've got the worst side of it and the best side of it.

"Beats, they definitely describe character," Björk says. **"Beats are how you walk down the street. Hip-hop people walk a certain way down a street, and you can see in the way they walk what kind of music they listen to. People that listen to funky '70s music, walk a certain way down the street. It's very much about the rhythm of your life and your lifestyle. The boys who program the beats with me say that I should try horseriding or crawling. Then maybe I would write either really fast songs or really slow ones."—Björk**

The worst side of it is to get really claustrophobic if they can't get enough oxygen. And if they go on top of a mountain and get very much oxygen. . . . In a way, singing is celebrating oxygen, because you're going [*takes a deep breath before wailing in careless random pitches*], "Aaaahhhh! Uuuuhhhh!"

Björk's had a long time to think about the effects of music on the human body. She recorded her first album, covers of Icelandic folk songs (and one instrumental original) at the age of 11 and has been involved in over 20 albums since. So she's had plenty of opportunity to build her own musical philosophies as they pertain to people. "Beats, they definitely describe character," Björk says. "Beats are how you walk down the street. Hip-hop people walk a certain way down a street, and you can see in the way they walk what kind of music they listen to. People that listen to funky '70s music, walk a certain way down the street. It's very much about the rhythm of your life and your lifestyle."

Her own lifestyle is far from conventional. A year ago, she tackled a journalist in a Bangkok airport, trying to protect her 12-year-old son, Sindri, from unwanted media attention. She broke up a public brawl between ex-boyfriends Tricky and Goldie in a New York club. Before recording *Homogenic*, she evaded a letter bomb sent to her London flat by an American fan (who then committed suicide). And yet she's clear-headed about issues of music, such as the welding together of electronic and acoustic instruments. She commands her fuzzy electronic beats to get along with the slurs of wood-resonating violins. But she draws the line when the synth patches disguise themselves as violins: "When plastic was invented, people wanted plastic to imitate marble, but I think plastic is great. Plastic can just be plastic. It's beautiful and kind of see-through. When it looks terrible is when it's trying to be wood or marble or whatever. That's how we humiliate these things we invent. We fancy something that is already quite conservative in our lives, because we haven't got imagination to invent new categories."

A plastic lawn chair ingrained with decals of fake wood knots won't fool an acute eye into believing it's seeing real wood. And songs created from prescribed formulas — forced out for the sake of a hit — won't fool a sharp, innovation-seeking ear into believing it's hearing a spectacular song. "Say you met a guy, and he's great for you," Björk hypothesizes. "If you've got 90 things on your list, he does all of them, but you just don't fancy him at all. So what are you gonna do? You're gonna look at him and make yourself love him? No, and that's the same with songs. If you believe in love — which I do so fiercely I could be arrested for it: It's an offense to love, because it's an individual force which goes its own way. I could never sit down and say, 'Okay, I'm waiting for that tune.' It's more like a reaction. You just walk around and you're trying to handle life."

"It's like, if you were to write a book about how to sleep," she says. "Obviously certain things would help, like having a bed and not having a very noisy environment. But you can't possibly decide what you're gonna dream and what movements you're gonna make. That's the same with songwriting. It's something stronger than you that just takes over."

puzzle-piece magician

Mixing exercise with work, Björk says she writes songs while her heart's at 90 bpm, speedwalking glassy-eyed down the street. "The boys who program the beats with me say that I should try horseriding or crawling," Björk laughs. "Then maybe I would write either really fast songs or really slow ones." Her past collaborators and producers have included such electronic warlocks as Massive Attack producer Nellee Hooper, 808 State's Graham Massey, Howie B, and Tricky.

This time she worked with an army of Marks — LFO's keyboardist/programmer Mark Bell, mixer Mark Stent, and engineer Markus Dravs. Björk counts on collaborating with people who speak her unique musical tongue: "I would describe what I wanted and then to bridge the gap between what I wanted and what it would become, I needed incredibly, outrageously brilliant technicians, because sometimes I was describing green hairy lumps and stuff like that. It takes a person with a sense of humor and imagination."

Björk doesn't complete arrangements and scores in her head while walking to the bus stop. She and *Homogenic* co-writer Mark Bell sometimes get to the studio without a game plan. But for Björk, songwriting is like getting eight hours of sleep or eating three meals a day: "It's an urge that you just have to do it or you go mad. If I don't sleep for a week I go a bit funny. If I don't eat for a week I go a bit funny. If I don't have sex for a week I go a bit funny. If I don't sing for a week I go a bit funny. It's just one of the most primitive functions of the body."

She averages about a song a month, as "a way of coping," she says. "It doesn't matter what I'm doing, if I'm working 900 hours a day, or if I'm on holiday. It's just a natural reaction to life for me," she says. She prefers to brainstorm about preproduction before she opens the studio door, which allows her to whiz through recording a song in one day. But before that, there's the long period of writing and revising. One day she'll say, "Okay, I think I've sussed it out." And the next evening she's apt to sigh, "No, I was completely wrong. I'm stupider than I thought. But now I think I've sussed it out, and tomorrow will be fine." This is where the walking comes in, after her anxiety meter clips and distorts. "If somebody says this, and then does that, and a woman comes in, and I do this. . . . And it doesn't make any sense," she says in a vague chatter of confusion. "Then I would walk, and a song comes out of it.

"But when I say this, it sounds like I know how to do it. Believe me, I don't, because that's another thing about love and songwriting which is similar. Just because you wrote a good song yesterday, there's absolutely no security that you will write one tomorrow. That's why we get addicted to it, because we never know."

soothsayer of fear and vision

After *Debut* and *Post*, "a collection of songs written over a period of 15 years," Björk claims her latest album reaches closer to the core of her persona. "I've got a rural energy that is quite Icelandic," she says. "I've got this kind of taste for hyper beauty." What transpires in *Homogenic* is more of her planet-transcending voice accompanied by a sparse shrubbery of synths set in a tundra of acoustic instruments. But *Homogenic* manages to hit dozens of emotional pinnacles with minimal instrumentation. Maybe it's the contrast between a layer of fuzzy beats leading to a rush of high-pitched violins next to ringing glass, airy saxophone samples, and her wide-open vocal chords. If you're not paying attention, you'll miss the weirdest little cameos of noises, like in "5 Years," the bizarre bit-part conversation among synths pretending to be ping-pong splats, a shaker of sand, and a hairdryer. Such dynamic minimalism calls for some attention to detail, like making dollhouse furniture. It also means self-control.

"I think it's sometimes good to tie your hands down, because it makes other parts of your body work more. But it's just a game. It's not a rule," Björk says. One part of the game was to refuse bass lines until the last moment, then squeeze them in: "I think bass lines are a feel-good factor, like, if there's a good bass line, nothing can go wrong. They're very cozy. A lot of the time you start with a bass line and the rest of the song comes. And if you refuse yourself of that, it makes you work harder in other areas."

Björk on songwriting: "It's like, if you were to write a book in your sleep. Obviously certain things would help, like having a bed and not having a very noisy environment. But you can't possibly decide what you're gonna dream about and what movements you're gonna make. That's the same with songwriting. It's something stronger than you that just takes over."—Björk

In her *Post* song "The Modern Things," Björk informs us that electrically charged objects, like cars, have always existed — "They've just been waiting in a mountain for the right moment." But she now suggests the electricity may have been right inside our own nervous systems, the whole time: "When acupuncture and needles are put in us, that's to trigger the electricity that's going through and around our body. So it's always been there. But I think people have always been afraid of progress. The minute when the monkey decided to become man, all the monkeys were going, 'Don't! Don't! We'll all die!' Then they invented fire, and they were like, 'Don't! We'll all burn!' And then of course they learned to cook." Björk, on the other hand, has never been one to fear progress. From music school starting at age six (playing piano and flute), she got the guts to sing, which led to writing melodies, then lyrics, arranging, and co-producing. With *Homogenic*, she became her own producer. "It doesn't really feel like a big jump," she shrugs. "I never thought, 'Oh my God, I'm a producer.'" Her song "Alarm Call" sums up Björk's easy resolve: "Today has never happened and it doesn't frighten me."

Contrary to the common belief that technology is incapable of conveying emotion, Björk is very comfortable with electric wizardry. "You can make a very warm song with a guitar, but you can also make a very cold song with a guitar. And with a computer you can make a very warm song, but also a very cold song. Computers don't represent the evil force from the future, like we're just numbers and we're all gonna wear uniforms, like George Orwell. If you find a song done with computers and electricity that has no feelings in it, that's because nobody put them there. You can't possibly blame the instrument."

Of course, technology can be a crutch. It allows you to pour a bunch of cool sounds on a DAT, walk onstage in a club, press play, cross your arms over your chest, and say, "Look, I'm a musician." You can produce a CD with a virtual 40-piece band without ever getting off the couch. But Björk doesn't view samplers and computers as a creative setback. "I think because we've got so many toys which are so exciting, we should make them more challenging for our minds and our hearts and our bodies, and take advantage of all this freedom we found." Here's where Björk comes in with her Nordic folklore talk, like a trollwife chanting magic spells: "It's just amazing. We can make noises that sound like three pink elephants and then go straight into the sound that's in your soul when it travels through your knee. You can improvise this, which is so much freedom."

[by Kylé Swenson, Keyboard, January 1998]

"There was no plan going into this," says Mark Bell, producer and keyboardist of LFO fame, who supplied much of *Homogenic's* electronic signature. "It was all unwritten. It was very natural. We didn't have any preconceived ideas of what we were going to do. I just brought over all my equipment, and then we messed about with it. I'd do something like, say, a drum part. Then she'd write something else over the top of it, and that would get me excited again. We'd build off each other."

And build they did. *Homogenic* is Björk at her bizarre best, as somber strings tangle with trash-truck techno. In the studio, samples were distorted, filtered, and manipulated in real time. Synths were sometimes played live, sometimes sequenced. And practically all the keyboards and drums were processed through rude stompboxes or effects.

Intrigued? Mark Bell takes us behind the scenes during the making of the record, and then the subsequent live performances.

How did you get the gig with Björk?

She first got in contact with me back in 1991, but we never actually worked together until this record. We kept in contact and talked over the years, and then I did some remixes for her ["Hyperballad" and "Possibly Maybe" from *Telegram*]. We were supposed to work together on *Debut* and *Post*, but that never happened. We were both really busy, and we just missed each other. But this time I went over to work with her for just, like, five days, to see how things would go — and those five days turned into five months.

This record came out surprisingly cohesive, especially when compared to Björk's previous two solo CDs.

Yeah. When I listen to songs from *Debut*, I really like it, but it does sound more like a collection of singles or stuff that's a bit more commercial. And then *Post* . . . that didn't do that much for me. But this one, you can tell that it's two people doing most of it. I mean, there's loads of different emotions, but it's still the same feeling And you can tell it's coming from the same general source.

Did the first song you worked on in the studio set the tone for the entire record?

"Hunter" was the first, so yeah. With Björk, she likes live instruments, but she can see the beauty of electronic things as well. When people say electronics have no soul, or whatever. . . . It's no different than any other instrument. Nothing has soul unless you play it, and she's always appreciated that. Like, with LFO, it's always been very over-the-top electronic, but also very human.

Describe how the songs came together, using "Hunter" as an example.

The drum machine was a [Roland TR-] 909, and the part was pretty complicated 'cause Björk did the vocals first, and then I listened to the lyrics — listened to how she phrased things — and then built the drum pattern around that.

I read that you often approach your tracks more like a traditional player — rolling tape and just going for it live, versus sequencing and editing.

Yeah. That drum pattern wasn't fine-tuned. I just played it, messing about with the filters live, in one take.

"It was real complicated just doing the actual drum patterns because of the timing, 'cause Björk had written the strings, and it would go for, like, seven beats, then 12 beats. So that's what was so hard — to try and make it sound smooth and flowing." —Mark Bell

So you'd be switching patterns on the fly and manipulating the knobs in real time?

Exactly. Changing patterns and controls like "snappy" [filter].

Did the two of you ever attempt to improvise and record simultaneously?

The songs "Pluto" and "Five Years" were done together like that.

Was most of the material conceived in the studio, or did either of you bring in pre-written ideas?

She'd written some string parts before, and then I wrote some chord structures when I got there, but the majority of it was the two of us messing about, really. Like, "Bachelorette" and "Five Years" were done before.

Can you describe the studio environment you worked in?

We went to Trevor Maurice's studio in Spain. He's a pretty famous drummer who's played with Kool And The Gang, and stuff like that. It was an amazing place on the side of this mountain. The actual studio didn't have loads of equipment — some [Tascam] DA-88s and a 24-track — but it was a really nice environment.

Other than the 909, what gear did you bring?

An old Casio FZ-10 sampler, an old Akai AX-80 keyboard, a Yamaha CS-15 analog, and a few guitar pedals, which a lot of the drum patterns went through.

What pedals did you use?

The Rat distortion pedal, a Boss RP-6 multi-effect, an [Electro-Harmonix] Electric Mistress — quite a lot of old pedals. They always add quite a lot of character to the noises.

Like the great underwater filter effects on "Joga."

Yeah, that was a few different pedals. How we did that one was, we just got the noises in the first place — some bass drums, snare drums, hi-hats, and we put them through the effects and then sampled them. It was real complicated just doing the actual drum patterns because of the timing. It was weird 'cause she'd written the strings, and it would go for, like, seven beats, then 12 beats. So that's what was so hard — to try and make it sound smooth and flowing.

Did you use a computer at any point during the sessions?

We used a Mac with [Emagic] Logic Audio, but we didn't use that much of the program. Just for sequencing, mainly. A lot of my things were done live, where things were being filtered and triggered by hand.

You're credited with "backwards accordion" on "Hunter." What's that all about?

[*Laughs.*] There's a man called Coba, a Japanese man who's this famous accordion player. He does Pepsi adverts, and things like that. But he came over, 'cause he knows Trevor [Maurice], and played a few parts. They were good, but they didn't really go with the songs. So I sampled it, cut it all up, messed about with it, and reversed some bits.

You're also credited with many of the album's synth bass lines.

I used a [Roland] SH-101 for those, mainly, and I'd just find rhythms that would go with the tracks. Like, say "Hunter.". . . I'd think of the rhythm of the words, and get the timing down first. Then I'd send that to the keyboard as a trigger, and just find the notes that went with it musically. Some of the other bass lines were just played in traditionally.

Were you involved in the mixing of this record?

I was there, but the man who mixed it was called Spike [Stent] — he mixes Depeche Mode and people like that. But I just wanted to make sure he didn't make it too . . . I don't know. I didn't trust anyone, even though he's very good. Björk was there as well; we both didn't want anyone to have a go at it without us being there.

Were most of the effects printed during mixdown, or did you record the original tracks wet?

Most of the effects were already on the tape when we mixed, really. So mixing was more about just getting the levels right. The challenging part about mixing is that you've heard the song so many times, and it's hard to be objective about the mix. So it was good to let him [Spike] go, and we'd leave the studio for a while. Then we'd come back in. Usually he'd just mess about with the levels, and he didn't feel like it needed many effects or anything. It was good how it worked out.

You performed with Björk and the string ensemble at the 1997 Tibetan Freedom Concert in New York. What was your approach to controlling the electronics onstage?

What we did was sample some parts, like the drum patterns, and I triggered them live. I have an [Akai] MPC-2000, and I'd press the pads and the rhythms would come in. Then I'd feed that through a Sherman Filterbank. A lot of it was like what we did in the studio.

Was there also a sequence running in the background, or was it all being triggered in real time by you?

There was always a basic song structure running, where all the noises would change for each part, but I was always triggering the sounds. I could ruin everything if I wanted. [*Laughs.*]

What gear were you using onstage, in addition to the Akai and Sherman?

A 909 through a filter, and a JD-800 for various noises. Like, there was a man who played the wine glasses on the song "All Neon Like." You know, when you move your finger around the top of the glass. So I resynthesized that noise, and played it on the JD-800.

Will you be going out on tour with Björk?

Yeah, I'm gonna be part of the American bit, but not the European one. They're coming up in a few weeks, but I'm just really tired at the moment.

Based on your experience at the Tibetan concert, do you think you'll keep your rig the same for future shows?

No. I want to do something different, but I still haven't decided exactly how I'm gonna do it yet. But I've been practicing different things at my studio. I want to bring the pedals [stompboxes] as well.

*[by Greg Rule, **Keyboard, January 1998**]*

roland tr-909

r hythm machines were among Roland's first products. At approximately the same time that Roland president Ikutaro Kakehashi foresaw the value of

vital stats

Description: The TR-909 was a hybrid of analog and digital circuits; other than PCM samples of hi-hat and ride and crash cymbals, all of its sounds were created via analog.

Production Dates: 1983-84.

Manufacturer: Roland Corporation, Osaka, Japan.

Approximate Number Made: 10,000.

Original Price: $1,195.

implanting a microprocessor in a rhythm machine, Roger Linn began developing the Linn LM-1, which — upon its release in 1980 — qualified as the first programmable drum machine that featured sampled sounds. Kakehashi wasn't prepared to abandon the use of analog sound generation in his rhythm instruments (namely the TR-808), even by the time the TR-909 was introduced in 1983. However, three of the 909's 11 percussion sounds — crash cymbal, ride cymbal, and hi-hat — were sampled. How long was the drum machine in production? A single year.

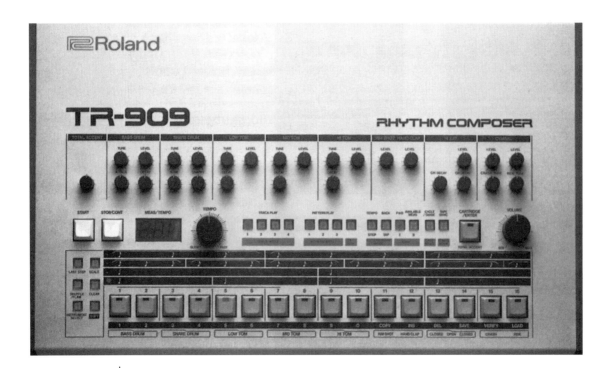

"We combined technologies to make a hybrid machine," Kakehashi explains. "The cymbal in the TR-909 was generated using digital technology, but the kick drum, snare, and other parts were made by analog circuits. We felt that was the best combination, but at that time everyone expected all sounds to be generated digitally. Digital had a better sound quality, and everybody liked to have all digital. Roger Linn developed his drum machine, which generated all of its drum sounds digitally. At that time, everyone wanted PCM, so that's why we couldn't continue to manufacture the TR-909. It was replaced in 1984 by a machine called the TR-707, which had all PCM sounds." Besides being notable for its hybrid sound-generation scheme, the 909 deserves credit for being Roland's first rhythm machine with MIDI.

Besides sporting three MIDI connectors (not the familiar in, out, and thru, but one MIDI in and two outs), the 909 also featured a DIN connector for synchronizing the machine with older Roland gear.

An improvement on the accents concept was also incorporated into the 909. Not only could you accent percussive events that occured on a particular beat, you could independently accent any sound. And by triggering 909 sounds from a MIDI controller, you could get a wider dynamic range.

Who Deserves Credit? Makoto Muroi, Chief Engineer of Roland's electronic drum and percussion division, provided the following information: Mr. Oue designed the TR-909's analog and PCM voice circuits, and Mr. Hoshiai developed its software.

However, Ikutaro Kakehashi prefers to give credit to design teams rather than singling out individuals. "The Japanese system takes teamwork, so there wasn't one person who was responsible. I think the concept to use a microcomputer was my idea, but the real development involved two or three people. Some people worked on the voicing, some people worked on the mechanical design. There wasn't just one person. This is quite different from the U.S. system. In the U.S., very clearly, 'I designed everything' is what many people say. But in Japan, no. So it's very difficult to say who did what. But it's very clear that Mr. Tadao Kikumuto designed the TR-909's hybrid concept. I think on the TR-808 as well. The concept and programming and hardware design were, in many cases, performed by different people."

[by Mark Vail, Keyboard, May 1994]

orbital

Plugged!

two days, eight bands, and 8,000-plus tweakers . . . Organic '96 was *the* electronic dance event of the year in the States. Held in California's lush San Bernardino National Forest and showcasing some of the best artists on the planet, *Orgasmic* '96 was more like it.

By winter, the Snow Valley resort is a haven for Southern California downhill skiers, but on this midsummer night, the site played host to a pack of rabid ravers who turned its grassy fields into a modern Dust Bowl. The smartest guy in the lot was the one dispensing dust-masks for a buck each. A short hike up the main ski trail, though, and it was pure heaven: panoramic mountain view, star-filled sky, and cosmic laser-beam swirls from below.

Back on Earth, there was no shortage of mind-altering experiences: There was the Brain Machine, the Space Ball, and other side-show attractions. The attendees were also an eyeful: drag queens with more face-paint than Tammy Faye Bakker (the winner wore a three-foot blonde beehive), grown men and women sucking pacifiers, and those ecstatic youngsters who kept their heads buried in the bass bins all night. Can you say hearing loss?

For us synth-lovin' types, the scenery — colorful as it was — took a backseat to the action onstage. If ever there were doubts about the health of synthesizers

Phil and Paul Hartnoll (collectively, Orbital). "It's a real family business," says Paul. "Knowing each other so well, it's easier to say 'that's crap,' and not have that weird ego thing."

◄..........................

on the live music front, this event should put them to rest. Not since Emerson and Downes in their prog primetime have we seen such mammoth synth rigs at a concert event. Orbital's horseshoe-shaped monster, in particular, looked like the mothership, and their show was unforgettable.

Taking the stage at 2:00 a.m., the stage awash with dry ice and Varilights, the brothers would have been invisible had it not been for their custom high-beam headlight visors. Like radioactive frogs bouncing behind banks of blinking hardware, Orbital doused the crowd with liquid electronica — a soothing contrast to the searing breakbeats cranked out by the Chemical Brothers.

Prior to the performance, it took a bit of arm-twisting to persuade the Hartnolls to do an interview; fresh off the plane from England, at the start of a hectic mini-tour of the U.S., they were much more interested in tucking into the free grub backstage than answering questions from the press. But we persisted, and after a brief intervention from press officer Sioux Z, and with the mellowing effects of their recently consumed dinner taking hold, we were granted an audience.

Taking advantage of the late afternoon sun and the spectacular view of the San Bernadino National Forest, we hiked up one of the dusty slopes, perched ourselves on top of a rock pile, fended off lizards, topless women, and security guards, and got down to business.

Where are you from?

Phil: From Sevenoaks, Kent [a small country town outside London].

What was your entry into music? Were you DJs?

Paul: Musicians, although we didn't play much of anything. I used to play the guitar, badly, and then we'd play it along with the electronics, fuzz pedals, wah-wah, that sort of thing. Then I gave up on the guitar.

Phil: I learned the saxophone for a while, dabbled around, but I wouldn't say I was a musician, I just had a real love for music.

Did you go out much, to clubs?

Phil: Not much really, not in Sevenoaks.

Paul: We did actually, that's a lie, because there was one place that was really good called the Grasshopper Inn. It was around 1986. That wave of rare groove stuff just before house kicked in, when it was all James Brown loops and hip-hop. And then around '88 or '89, house started coming there as well.

So you received a pretty broad musical education through that club?

Paul: Yeah and also from a friend who used to do pirate radio, and had the largest collection of Chicago house you're ever likely to see.

Did you find that you had to move out of Sevenoaks at some point?

Phil: I moved to London and did silly jobs up there for a while. Paul stayed in Kent.

Paul: I stayed for a while. Our parents left to run a pub down the road and I stayed. Around that time we were collecting more musical equipment. It wasn't

Gear galore. Few techno artists have been able to recreate their recordings on-stage with as much energy and excitement as Orbital.

really feasible to have a studio in a paper-thin-walls flat in London, and we had spare bedrooms in Sevenoaks where we could put a studio. I was appreciating living in the country too then, with the aid of cannabis.

What kind of gear did you start out with?

Paul: The first thing we had was this Latin percussion drum machine — a Korg. It was a little silver thing.

Do you still have it?

Phil: Oh yeah it's still there in the studio.

Paul: Then Phil bought a Poly-800, so we used to play about with those two and my guitar. Then he got a 707; he had to sell his sax to get that, but the electro bug had caught on in our house. This was about 1985, when electro was big, industrial funk, stuff on Factory Records out of Manchester. . . . Then Phil decided to go to America, and he lent his keyboards to a friend *instead of leaving them with me!*

Phil: I didn't really think. This person just asked me, so I said yes.

Paul: It didn't really matter though, because I had some money, and I was able to buy a drum machine and keyboard of my own. I'll tell you what happened, I decided I wanted to get a [Sequential] Six Trak. The idea of six sequences, a six-part multitimbral thing, I thought was great. In Soho Soundhouse I saw that as well as the 707. They were selling the Roland 909s for $400. I could afford both, but I was told by the sales assistant, "Oh no, you can't run Roland and Sequential Circuits MIDI stuff together. MIDI only talks to the same company." Basically the idiot couldn't figure out how to sync up the two things. So being completely wet behind the gills, I bought the Poly-800 knowing that was a good keyboard, and I got the 909, but I was very dubious about it 'cause it wasn't as good as the 707, *or so I thought*. When Phil got back from America, we put his stuff together with mine. Him lending his stuff to someone else turned out to be a good thing because it forced me to get my own stuff.

Where did you go in America?

Phil: I was in Manhattan mainly, in search of hip-hop culture. I thought I would find all the records, all the culture, but it wasn't really like that. I did tape a lot of good music from the radio — KISS FM live mixes, stuff like that. When house really started hitting, we didn't find it that unusual really.

Paul: It just sounded like electro and Hi-NRG combined.

At what point did you lay your first viable pieces of music down?

Paul: I bought a four-track early on, so I was making tons of tapes back then. We've been 12 years dabbling in home recording, but it's hard to point to a time when those recordings became viable. Early on we weren't sending our stuff around. We felt it wasn't ready, but eventually some friends of mine took a couple of tracks to this DJ who did a radio show — Jack Man Jay, his real name is Kevin Marsh — and he took them to Jazzy M, who used to do London Wicked Radio. He played them. That's when we really started taking tapes around.

Were you always called Orbital?

Paul: I had a couple of tracks under the name DS Building Contractors.

And the first Orbital release?

Paul: Was in 1989: *Chime* on London Records.

At what point did you come into contact with sampling?

Paul: After we were burgled, and they stole loads of our stuff. With the insurance money we bought an [Akai] S700 sampler.

You were self-taught?

Paul: Yeah, there was no one else to teach us.

Let's fast-forward to In Sides. You've gone for some very organic sounds. Is that a dulcimer we're hearing on "The Box"?

Paul: Yeah. We actually approached it as trying to make a record that was shorter. We're a little sick of the overall playing time of an album being 74 minutes instead of 45. I think it can work better shorter. So we thought, let's do a shorter album, lots of tracks, much more up-tempo, much more dancey, really jolly — and of course that didn't happen at all. We go into the studio with

"We thought, let's do a shorter album, lots of tracks, much more up-tempo, much more dancey, really jolly — and of course that didn't happen at all. We go into the studio with an idea, and often it turns out completely different." —Paul Hartnoll, Orbital

an idea, and often it turns out completely different, but that doesn't matter. That is a dulcimer sample. We sampled four different notes and then split the notes onto two sides of the keyboard so you can play them with your fingers like a real dulcimer. We did things like velocity to start point and velocity to pitch point and velocity to filter — which vary ever so slightly so the sound is more natural.

So you spend a lot of time crafting the sounds and samples?

Paul: Yeah, it's important with the dulcimer, for example, because if you just had it on a regular keyboard it wouldn't sound authentic.

Define each of your roles in the studio process. Is it a 50/50 split, or do you each specialize in certain aspects?

Paul: I specialize in holding the mouse.

And Phil specializes in trying to get it off you?

[*Much laughter all 'round.*]

Paul: We both specialize in staring at the screen and discussing everything. What often happens is we have two keyboards up and running, and I'll be fiddling around with chords while Phil might be working on a lead. All of a sudden it'll be ahh, stop, do that again, and we'll work it out like that.

What kind of drum sounds do you favor?

"We both specialize in staring at the screen and discussing everything. What often happens is we have two keyboards up and running and I'll be fiddling around with chords while Phil might be working on a lead. All of a sudden it'll be ahh, stop, do that again, and we'll work it out like that." —Paul Hartnoll, Orbital

Paul: I enjoy breakbeats and I enjoy drum machines; I just enjoy it all, but with this album we got a friend of ours, Cloone, who is a drummer and put him in a big studio, which we never normally hire, and recorded him on 15 different mikes, onto an ADAT, and some other DATs.

Playing to a click track?

Paul: Sometimes, although being a drummer he doesn't like playing to a click. So we got a day of him drumming so we could make our own breakbeats, which is enjoyable because you really have to work to make it sound dynamic. It was fun to be able to take the bass drum out or put it in really loud or with reverb. We also just got an 808, because we couldn't stand to be without it any longer. We used to have to borrow one, but we had to have our own. So that turns up a lot beside Cloone's breaks.

Did you tell him what type of beat you wanted him to play, or did you leave it up to him?

Paul: Well, he kept asking us, and we just said do what you like. We did get him to use brushes and a couple of different snares.

Phil, take us through your studio setup for this record.

Phil: Oh God, there were a lot of samples on this record.

Paul: No there weren't, not that many. The [Oberheim] Xpander shows up a lot, the ARP 2600 has a nice airing this time. The Roland modular turned up on this album as well.

[*At this point the technological discussion is interrupted when Phil spots a gecco on a rock, and a naked woman sunbathing a few yards away. After much craning of necks we continue.*]

Did you use any modeling synths like the Clavia Nord Leads or Korg Prophecies?

Paul: Yeah we have a Prophecy, but we didn't get it in time to use it on this album.

And the sequencing?

Paul: We use [Emagic] Logic Audio, which is fine except it can't handle long tracks the way we do them; we have to do tracks in four chunks. I don't know what's wrong exactly, we've had a lot of people come and look at it but no one seems to be able to figure it out. We might have to send it to the big man.

How many albums are you on now?

Paul: Four.

Phil: Seven. We've got a seven-album deal of which we've made four.

What gear do you use onstage?

Phil: Oh, blimey.

Paul: We've got three [Alesis] MMT-8s, with two spares because I have to change one halfway through the set. They have shit memory.

Do you use them for their supposed feel?

Paul: Yeah, the feel is really tight, and I like the way you can turn them on and off and then have the same thing in there, like a drum machine. We've also got an [E-mu] e64, an EIII, a [Roland] Jupiter-6, R-70, 808, 909, and R-8, a [Novation] Bass Station, a Prophecy, and an Xpander.

You're brave to take that old beast on the road.

Paul: It's been very reliable actually, apart from freaking out a couple of times in Europe.

To what extent are you able to improvise?

Paul: Well with the MMT-8s in pattern mode, you can go four bars, eight bars, 64 bars — it completely varies and we just punch things in and out. You get quite good at it. You get to learn what works. You can end up using mutes and MIDI echo to create breaks that aren't really there.

How would you describe the experience of translating a studio venture onto the live stage?

Phil: A pain in the fucking arse.

Paul: The only way you can do it is in real time. I make a line of phantom folders and put them in order 'til I have the whole set there, backed up about a thousand times.

Are you happy with where your career has taken you?

Phil: Oh yeah.

Paul: It's more than I ever dreamed of. I always thought it would be great to be as culty as Cabaret Voltaire.

Give us an insight into what it's like working with family.

Paul: Well, we don't know what it's like working without family. Our Mum does our books, so it's a real family business. Knowing each other so well, it's easier to say, "that's crap," and not have that weird ego thing.

What do you hope to do in the future?

Paul: Film soundtracks, definitely. We've had a few tracks in films, but I want to write the whole bloody score. I hope you're listening, Terry Gilliam.

Despite battling severe Dust Lung and sleep deprivation, the *Keyboard* posse took in all but a few final minutes of the Organic extravaganza. And what a show it was. With nary a technical hiccup, mosh-pit melee, or pop-star temper tantrum, good vibes prevailed (despite the negative effects of the above-mentioned lung affliction and non-organic food).

With the Orb cranking away in the background, and the morning sun just around the corner, we packed our battered bags, slammed in a tape of London DJ Giles Petersen's *Vibrazone* radio show, and hit the highway back to San Francisco. Winding over the mountain pass, it was all this driver could do to keep the rented hot-rod between the lines. Caffeine and toothpick eye-props were the name of the game. Not counting the coyotes and jackrabbits darting across the road, our car was the only moving object in sight for miles. Surreal, to say the least. Pure *Hills Have Eyes*.

[by Caspar Melville and Greg Rule, Keyboard, October 1996]

roland tr-808

*i*ntroduced in 1980, Roland's TR-808 analog drum machine didn't really become notable until it had long been out of production. Its popularity soared in the 1990s, thanks to techno and hip-hop music. The TR-808 became so popular, in fact, that you can find renditions or imitations of its sound in all kinds of contemporary sample libraries, synth sound sets, and emulation software such as Steinberg's popular ReBirth.

vital stats

Description: Step-time programmability was one of the TR-808's claims to fame, along with its distinguished analog sound.
Production Dates: 1980-83
Manufacturer: Roland Corporation, Osaka, Japan.
Approximate Number Made: 12,000
Original Price: $1,195.

Five percussion sounds characterize the state of the 808: the hum kick, the ticky snare, the tishy hi-hats (open and closed), and the spacy cowbell. Low, mid, and high toms, congas, a rim shot, claves, a handclap, maracas, and cymbal fill out the 808's sonic complement. The accent function — integral, as Roland president Ikutaro Kakehashi pointed out, in making the automatic rhythm machine musically useful — survived the transition from the earlier CR-78 to the new machine.

Roland's TR-808 drum machine. Orbital bought one in 1996, "because we couldn't stand to be without it any longer. We used to have to borrow one, but we had to have our own."

Thanks to its front-panel layout, which included a graphic design to help the user visualize metric divisions of a pattern's measures, the TR-808 was easier to program. In addition, it allowed step programming of patterns. "The step-writing interface wasn't so new," Kakehashi says, "but it was the first time that we paid more attention to the people who program in real time. It used to be that our customer was the home-organ player. Then people in the music industry started to pay attention to our rhythm machines. Such a musician was agreeable to programming by himself. That's why we developed the step-writing system, so you could slow the tempo down, enter your rhythm events, and then speed it up and hear the realistic rhythm pattern that you had just created."

Besides its improved sound and programmability, the 808 incorporated a number of groundbreaking features, including volume knobs for each voice, multiple audio outputs, and the immediate precursor to MIDI. On the rear of the 808 — as well as other 1981-vintage, pre-MIDI Roland rhythm machines (the CR-8000 and TR-606), the TB-303 Bass Line, and the EP-6060 electronic piano (which featured an arpeggiator) — you'll find a five-pin DIN jack that a standard MIDI plug will fit into. MIDI, however, it isn't. Although this connector was for synchronizing devices, Mr. Kakehashi asserts that there is a reason for the similarity between this and MIDI connectors.

"We had developed our own communications protocol," he explains. "Inside, it was the same as today's MIDI. At the same time, Sequential Circuits was developing a MIDI-like protocol. We called ours the DCB Bus, they called theirs by another name. Then we started discussing how to develop a common standard. Eventually MIDI came out, but actually more than 80 or 90% of it was based on the DCB Bus. Of course, I don't want to say that everything was developed by Roland, because that isn't fair. It was a joint effort. Both companies agreed to implement the best ideas from both companies, so we jointly created MIDI. But when you compare it with the DCB Bus, you can see how similar they are."

Just as many people would love to see the Ford Motor Company remanufacture the '57 T-bird, there are those who speculate that, were Roland to make more TR-808s, the analog beat box would outsell all of its digital competitors.

Who deserves credit? Makoto Muroi, Chief Engineer of Roland's electronic drum and percussion division, provided the following information: Mr. Nakamura designed the analog voice circuits for both the CR-78 and TR-808. Mr. Matsuoka developed the TR-808's software.

[by Mark Vail, Keyboard, May 1994]

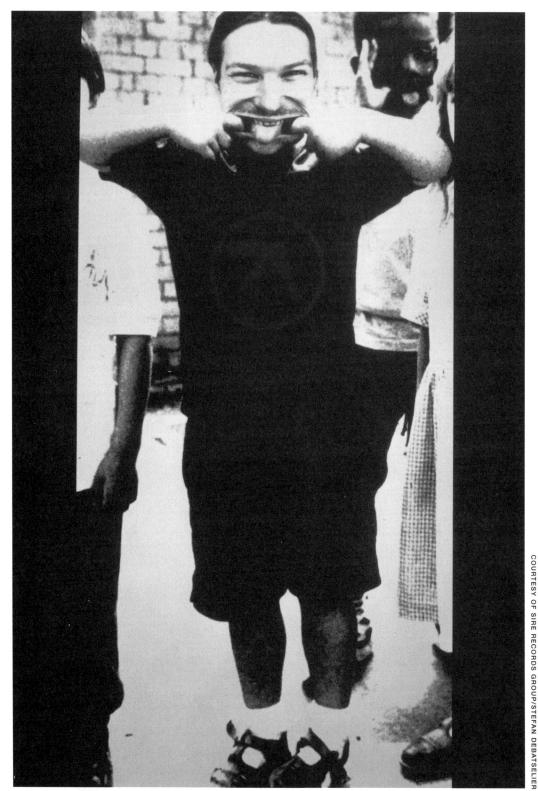

COURTESY OF SIRE RECORDS GROUP/STEFAN DEBATSELIER

aphex twin

Weird Science

On record he's known as Aphex Twin and sometimes Polygon Window, but many in the industry prefer to think of him as the mad scientist of electronica. Richard James has designed and built his own oddball electronic instruments from scratch, and has influenced countless electro musicmakers along the way.

Sampling continues to play an integral part in what James and artists like him do. So more than a few of us were curious to learn what type of material he samples, how he manipulates his data, what he thinks of the current crop of machinery, and whether he thinks it's acceptable to sample passages from other artists.

Somewhat surprisingly, James revealed a general dissatisfaction with the state of technology, summarizing samplers as "shit. I could talk for ages about all the things they should have on them that they don't." And when it comes to sampling material from other artists, or being sampled, James said he didn't care if someone copied his whole track and put it out under a different name.

Here then, straight from the mouth of James, are candid comments on the state of samplers and sampling.

Richard James, one of the most outspoken (and photogenic) artists in electronica.
◀·····························

"Today's samplers, they're just s—t, really. I designed and built my own sampler for a college project once. When it worked, I reckon it pissed on just about any manufactured sampler."

How did you get into sampling?

I started out making tape samples until I eventually got one of those kits from Synclair — one of those build-it-yourself things for about 50 pounds. That's what got me hooked on sampling.

How do you marry samplers with your homemade instruments?

I use samplers mainly because the gear that I build doesn't respond to MIDI. I have to sample the sounds and use them that way sometimes to get a tighter feel. If I trigger all the stuff I've made with voltages, it has a looser kind of feel. So I use the sampler for tightness, really.

Describe the ideal sampler.

It would be a sampling workstation of sorts, but it would be portable and it would run off batteries. Nothing like that is out there; the closest things might be the [Akai] MPC-60 and [Sequential] Studio 440. But today's samplers, they're just shit, really. I designed and built my own sampler for a college project once. When it worked, I reckon it pissed on just about any manufactured sampler. I could talk for ages about all the things they should have on them that they don't.

For example?

Too many samplers today are made like DAT machines. Manufacturers don't put enough features on them, probably 'cause they think it'll scare off the users; they think there are probably too many buttons on the thing already.

What features do you think should be standard?

Totally variable sampling rates. You should be able to sample from, say, zero to 100kHz. Instead, they give you four or five rates. You should be able to do loads of digital effects.

Could you give us some examples of the types of things you've sampled of late?

Well, I'll have to be a prick about that.

Excuse me?

I don't like to talk about the way I do tracks.

So you won't tell us about the "Tampax" sample?

All right, but that's just a really boring example of sampling. I nicked a bit of a Tampax advertisement, and used it in a track. But I don't want to say anything about the way I use it.

Why not?

In this business, it's kind of a geeky kind of music world where everyone thinks their success depends upon their secrets of the trade. In actual fact, it probably doesn't depend on that at all, but I still get chills down my spine thinking about telling people about the way I do things, so I don't.

[*Note: James wasn't kidding. When we tried to get an up-close look at his bizarre electronic instruments during soundcheck, we were promptly escorted off the stage.*]

Okay, let's approach the subject from another angle. Did you have to get permission from the Tampax company before using that sample?

No. The things I've sampled . . . I've probably only sampled about three or four things ever that haven't been my own material. The last 14 months, I haven't used anyone else's equipment, never mind anyone else's sounds. I just became totally obsessed with using my own sounds, and got to the point where I chucked out all my standard gear in my studio. Now I exclusively use my own gear, apart from things like computers and samplers. But everything that makes a sound, basically, is my own gear.

What do you feel should happen in the courts concerning sampling rights?

I don't care. I don't care if someone copies my whole track and puts it out under a different name.

Really?

Absolutely.

[by Greg Rule, Keyboard, May 1994]

Richard James is one of the most brilliant (and bizarre) electronic musicmakers on the planet. But how in the world does he find time to record, tour, *and* build his own instruments? Filter boxes, drum machines, custom keyboard modifications, and even a sampler — there isn't much he hasn't tried. As of 1997, he hadn't changed a bit. Richard was still a tinkering maniac, but his focus had shifted from hardware to software.

"I've got three Macs," he revealed, "two laptops and a Power PC. I use all the sequencers on the market, but at the moment I've been solely using my own program to create new algorithms." And not with Opcode's Max. He'd been building the algorithms from scratch. "It's like using a programming language. A bit like Pascal. I've been doing it for about three months, so it's all quite primitive, but it's looking really interesting. This language . . . you can bring in your own samples and mess around with them. And it's got DSP functions you can't get anywhere else, but you have to program it in. There's no fancy sliders, although they're easy to construct. I've made loads of graphical interfaces for things.

"The algorithm I just finished," he continued, "is a percussion thing that lets you swap and change the sounds. It does bass as well, but it's really acidy. You can leave it on for, like, an hour, and it really comes up with some mad shit. I made it learn to gradually change [the music] over time."

While he didn't plan to market his software, he had been showing it off at gigs. "I just finished a tour, and I used it for one of the tracks. It was pretty interesting watching people dance to my algorithm." His touring rig consisted of, get this, "One laptop computer, a little mixer, and an effects unit. But soon I'll be eradicating the mixer and effects. So basically it'll be one computer. It does everything I did before with live samples and sequences. I've put every element down on a digital track [in Digidesign's Pro Tools], so I can mix between tracks."

Speaking of Pro Tools, "It's wicked," he enthused. "You don't notice it's there, which is what you want with computers. It doesn't get in your way." While he purchased most of the third-party plug-ins for it, Richard, true to his tinkering image, also created one from scratch. "Within about two weeks I came up with one with this programming language I've been using. It's really, really cool. You can loop between sections, and loop individual tracks the same way you could

"I've been into breakbeat culture ever since it started, through hip-hop, hardcore, and jungle. So I've always been into nicking other things, recycling 'em, basically mashing 'em up and making something different. I just like to mash things up a bit more than most people, that's all."

with a sequencer. And I've got this thing on there so you can resynthesize each track, change its pitch. . . ."

Talking to Richard about his homemade software almost derailed me from the main purpose of the interview: to discuss his self-titled album on Sire. *Richard D. James* is like nothing I'd heard before — a bizarre 15-song blend of feeble synth sounds and jagged jungle loops. "Most of the album was done on my Mac, basically. Even the keyboard sounds were all pretty much computer-generated. Native audio." And when Richard sings, the sound gets even weirder. Give "Milkman" a spin, for example. "That was modulated on the computer," he said of the twisted vocal track.

Richard's drum programming is particularly impressive — rife with triplets and unpredictable stops and starts. "I think the main influence is Luke [Vibert] from Wagon Christ. He really inspired me to get into it more. I used to do lots of crazy triplets and stuff at a slower pace, but he really got me into doing it at a faster pace. He gave me the spark to do it faster, but now I'm trying to take it to all extremes, basically."

Richard's jungle influence comes from "any of the drum 'n' bass and breakbeat-artists. It's nothing new to me. I've been into breakbeat culture ever since it started, through hip-hop, hardcore, and jungle. So I've always been into nicking other things, recycling 'em, basically mashing 'em up and making something different. I just like to mash things up a bit more than most people, that's all."

One of his favorite mashing tools is Steinberg's ReCycle. "Yeah, it's quite a wicked program. The most useful thing about it is it creates a bank on your sampler, and gives it loads of sample names. And that saves you an hour, at least. You can cut something up into, like, 90 samples, and transfer it over SCSI in a minute. That would take two hours normally."

And not just for breakbeats, Richard uses ReCycle for melodic material as well. "I might play a violin or a trumpet scale into Pro Tools — every note I can think of — and then bang it into ReCycle, chop it up into little bits, bang it into the sampler, and you've got a complete bank of sounds in your sampler in about five minutes."

Richard and his laptop toured the U.K., but he hopes to circle the States in the future. "This is the next step for me," he says of his strange new sound. "It's like the first step for a much bigger step that I hope to take later on."

[by Greg Rule, Keyboard, April 1997]

steinberg recycle

S ampled loops are the foundation of many modern musical styles. A loop can give a track a hypnotic "electro-organic" quality that can't be simulated with drum machines or sequencers/sound modules. The biggest limitation of sampled loops, though, is that they're pretty much set in stone. If the tempo or the feel is wrong for a given song, the songwriter or producer faces an unappetizing menu of choices — change the song, find a new loop, tune the loop to a new pitch, or try to time-stretch the sample to fit. Time-stretching DSP algorithms are getting better, but they still produce sonic artifacts, and even after a loop is time-stretched, it's still set in stone. It triggers from the start and plays straight through, the same every time — great if what you want is obsessive repetition, but not so great if you'd like to throw listeners a few curves.

If you're familiar with this scenario, you'll understand how useful a program like ReCycle can be. With ReCycle, a rhythm loop is no longer a fixed entity.

vital stats

Production Dates: 1994-present
Manufacturer: Steinberg
Description: Sampled rhythm loop editing software.
Original Price: $199.

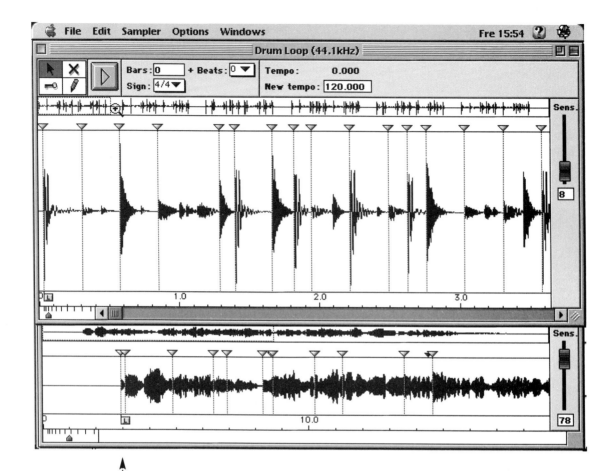

It slices, it dices, it turns digital audio inside out: Steinberg's ReCycle editing software has changed the face of electronic musicmaking, especially in the worlds of jungle and drum 'n' bass.

Not only can you speed the loop up or slow it down, you can change the feel by editing the timing of certain drum hits. You can edit out some of the sounds entirely and replace them with others, retune the snare without affecting the pitch of the kick, pan one drum within a loop to a separate audio output for some special processing, add stuttering effects, juggle the order of the notes, or take a smooth-feeling groove and quantize it rigidly so that it does the robot stomp.

But that's not all. You can derive a groove from a sample and then apply it to whatever you'd like, even if you don't own a sampler. This program makes it practical for the first time to quantize MIDI to audio or vice-versa — or to quantize one chunk of audio to the events in another chunk.

Performing this magic is a snap, which is exactly the point. ReCycle doesn't actually do anything that you couldn't do yourself with your sampler's and sequencer's editing commands, but it does in five minutes what would otherwise take an hour or more — and it does it perfectly, with no guesswork. ReCycle operates strictly in the time domain, not in the frequency domain, so it can't split apart events that occur simultaneously. Thus, to use the example mentioned above, you can retune the snare drum without affecting the kick only if the two never fall on the same beat.

ReCycle performs, in an integrated fashion, four basic tasks. First, it loads a sample file, either from the computer hard disk or over SCSI from your sampler. Presumably, this file contains the audio that you want to loop. Second, it looks for peaks in the audio waveform and makes some educated guesses about where the beats are in the loop. It doesn't require a huge sharp peak to find a beat, only a place where the amplitude rises noticeably. (In fact, we're told that the analysis algorithm doesn't just find peaks; it's more sophisticated than that.) If you don't like the program's guesses, you're free to edit the beat markers, adding new ones of your own and hiding some or all of the existing ones. Third, it splits the wave file into a number of separate chunks based on the positions of the markers (also known as "slice points"), and transmits these chunks to your sampler as separate samples. Along with the individual samples, it creates and transmits a program (keymap, envelopes, etc.) for the sampler that assigns these samples to the keyboard. Finally, it creates a Standard MIDI File that, when loaded into any sequencer, will send note-ons to the sampler in such a way as to trigger the individual samples in order. When this MIDI file plays back, the sound coming out of the sampler should be virtually identical to the original loop, even though the sound is now coming from a number of separate "time slices."

ReCycle has almost single-handedly spawned new dance music genres. Creators of the signature sliced/diced drum 'n' bass (jungle) drum patterns, in particular, owe an enormous debt of gratitude to this ingenious piece of software.

[by Jim Aikin, Keyboard, September 1994. Additional text by Greg Rule.]

mark snow
of the x-files

Cutting-Edge Synth Goes Prime Time

So what business does a soundtrack composer have being in a book about electronic pop music? Simple. Mark Snow is one of the most prolific and inspirational electronic music artists of the decade. His music is aimed more at the subliminal side of the electro spectrum, but everything he does is the product of a Synclavier and a rack of synths. Each week, Snow's music wafts into millions of homes via one of television's hottest properties: *The X-Files*.

More than a hit TV show, *The X-Files* has become a way of life for its rabid, loyal followers. X-Philes, as they're often called, are the new Trekkies. And it's easy to see why so many have bought in: *The X-Files* is a well-written, well-produced, well-acted knockout. FBI agents Fox Mulder (portrayed by actor David Duchovny) and Dana Scully (Gillian Anderson) forge weekly into the unexplained, unknown, and unexpected, and their spooky adventures are made all the more scintillating by surreal, ambient musical soundtracks and dynamic sound effects.

Which is where Snow fits in. While many television shows employ full orchestras for the musical trackwork, Snow does it all in his Santa Monica, California, home studio — a peaceful, inconspicuous contrast to the Hollywood soundstage.

As composer for *The X-Files*, Mark Snow delivers electronic music to millions each week. Says show creator/producer Chris Carter: "Whenever I go to the conventions, and whenever I go online, huge compliments are always paid to Mark about the music."

◄ ·······················

I spent an action-packed day onsite with *The X-Files* crew, watching Episode #10 of the 1995/96 season being whipped into shape. Now it's your turn to take a peek backstage. First, sit in on a high-level meeting as Snow plays his new score for the show's producers. Then go one-on-one with each of the five interviewees as they describe the process of writing, recording, and mixing the music and sound effects. Sprinkled throughout are bits of insider information that relate to visual effects, logistics, creative processes, and the like.

act 1
the meeting

Five of *The X-Files'* top brass have joined Mark Snow at his home studio to evaluate this week's score. Along with Snow, I'm rubbing elbows with creator/executive producer Chris Carter, co-executive producer Howard Gordon, co-producer Paul Rabwin, writer Frank Spotnitz, and sound supervisor Thierry J. Couturier.

Today's meeting is called the Music Playback Session, but for Snow it might as well be the Nail-Biting Session. He's been cranking away for the past three days on what amounts to 35-plus minutes of music — a major load for a 43-minute show, not counting commercials. If the producers don't like what they hear, Snow must write, record, and mix new material that day. Gulp.

Here's how it went. . . .

Monday, 8:30 a.m. Before business, the crew congregates in the kitchen for coffee and conversation. Chris Carter has just flown in from an *X-Files* book signing session in New York. He brings good news: Last week's show held up surprisingly well against the rival network's much-publicized Princess Diana interview. High fives are exchanged, and the conversation quickly turns to aliens, lepers, the end of the world, and the like. Major TV executives discussing alien abductions — gotta love it.

9:00. The scene shifts to the backyard studio. Chitchat subsides as Snow, seated at his Synclavier and Macintosh, fires up the first cue. It's a powerful scene — a mass humanoid execution — and the music is equally powerful: schizophrenic strings meet roof-rattling orchestral hits. All watch, bug-eyed.

The truth is in here: Mark Snow's Santa Monica home studio, where he creates *X-Files* soundtracks with a Synclavier and rack of synth modules.

9:04. Cue ends. The consensus is "spectacular," but Carter has reservations about the overall mood. "It's a bit too triumphant," he says. "I think it needs something a little darker, more disturbing." "More minor sustained chords," adds Gordon, jokingly. Snow takes notes. Meanwhile, Carter and Rabwin discuss darkening the color of a close-up shot. "The leper's makeup looks a little obvious in that light," observes Carter. Rabwin grabs his notepad, and agrees to have the scene darkened later that day.

9:08. There's a minor Synclavier hiccup, but Snow pounces on it and quickly the system is back in sync. As the raw video plays, unaccompanied, Carter speaks out: "I'm assuming there's some music here. This feels very cue-y to me." Mark whispers, "Whenever there's a problem with missing music, I'm off the hook." True, since Snow is uninvolved in the spotting process. F.Y.I., spotting is when the show's music editor views the raw footage and decides where music should be placed. Jeff Charbonneau spots *The X-Files* (We'll hear more from him later).

9:13. The next cue plays. This time the setting is a rundown research lab that's become a hideout for lepers. Unlike typical TV music that stops and starts from scene to scene, Snow's music often flows through scene changes, and this cue is no exception. At the end, Carter nods to Snow. Snow nods back. Translation: Two nods equal job well done. Next.

9:20. This cue is particularly long and dramatic. Scully visits the mass grave site with one of the lepers, but when a helicopter suddenly appears overhead, the two scramble into the woods. Tension mounts as a small army of ground and air commandos bears down. All seems well with Snow's music until the helicopter buzzes back into the picture, prompting Carter to say, "Whoa. Stop. I like the strings up to the point where the helicopter comes down. Maybe you can let the music go out, let the helicopter take over, then bring it back in." Snow takes notes. A beeper goes off, and there's a brief break in the action. "Did anyone hear the new Beatles song? . . . "

9:25. The studio phone rings. It's one of the show's executives on the line. There's been a last-minute timing change in the first cue. A discussion breaks out. Snow doesn't seem too concerned about the powwow. "They picked the right cue to change," he says. It is, after all, the same one that needs a musical makeover anyway.

9:28. The next cue is a barn-burner: Crash! Boom! Bang! Snow's percussive hits are rattling the walls. In general, there's not much melodic material to be found in *X-Files* soundtracks, and purposely so (as you'll read later in the Chris Carter segment). Says Snow: "Melodic cues happen only once in maybe 30 or so."

9:32. The music continues, but evolves. During one suspenseful moment, a rattling sound fades in, then out. Snow uses this sample on several occasions during the episode, along with slow, ambient string lines and hollow, icy synth textures. These stark, wet sounds complement the deep black and blue images onscreen.

9:37. Cue ends. "Excellent," says Carter, nodding. Snow nods back. Phone rings.

9:45. The next cue starts. A train barrels down the tracks with a bomb onboard, and it's ticking down to blastville. Big, psychotic string crescendos and loud, percussive bangs ring out. Eventually we see a fireball, and Snow's music takes a sudden turn from adrenaline to sadness.

9:52. When the cue ends, chatter erupts. Carter gives Snow a nod. Rabwin and Couturier discuss the timing of a certain metallic sound effect.

9:57. Before departing, Carter makes a proposal to the group. The current tag line that accompanies the main title is: "The Truth is Out There." Carter suggests it be changed to: "Apology is Policy." The group seems to like it, and the change is made.

With the meeting over, it's time to go one-on-one with the team members. Since Chris Carter has a pressing engagement, he's the first victim.

act 2
creator/producer CHRIS CARTER

What led to the hiring of Mark Snow?

When we started, all anyone had seen was the temp score Jeff Charbonneau had put together for the pilot so I, of course, had to go out and get a composer. I ended up interviewing a lot of people, and listening to piles of tapes. Bob Goodwin, who was a friend of Mark's from way back, suggested I talk to Mark. So I came over here and I liked him very much. I liked his music. I liked his attitude. I liked the fact that he lived close to me. And so I decided to just push the button with Mark. I think he'll tell you that I'm very, very hands-on. I get very involved. Even though my music vocabulary is not from a musician's tongue, I understand how music goes to picture, and how to play emotions.

After we did the pilot, I'd heard the temp score so many times. . . . We'd won with that score, and I think I was afraid to vary too far from it. What Mark did was give me the flavor of the temp, but he gave it his own signature, as well.

Mark said he had to write and rewrite the theme song several times before you signed off on it.

[*Grins.*] Yeah, he'd send me things, and I'd say, "No, not like that. More like this." And he'd send me something, and I'd say, "No, not like that. More like this." We went through this long process, and he'd send me all kinds of stuff. And then one day — whether or not this had a direct effect — I sent him a Smiths song that had a sort of mournful guitar in it. I think that might have reflected back in our theme. I thought, "This is a great theme," because first of all, it wasn't really a melodic, hummable little tune, yet I could image every Boy Scout troop on their camp-out, sitting around the campfire whistling it.

It has sort of a *Twilight Zone*-type of effect.

It does, although it doesn't have the obvious hook of [sings *Twilight Zone* hook line] "du-du-dudu, du-du-dudu." But it had something a little more moody and dark and meandering, and I liked that.

Did you know that was the one the minute you heard it?

He sent me three versions of it. When I heard the first one, I thought, "That's pretty cool." Then I listened to the next version and thought, "That's also cool." Then the third version, "Don't like that one as much." So I picked one of those. He remixed it a little bit and we had our theme. Since then, though, it's been almost magically easy with Mark because he gets the show. First out, I wanted the music to be real Philip Glass — minimal, textural, but with those repeating phrases — and Mark steered me a little bit away from that. But he really settled into it.

There is certainly a musical signature from show to show.

Yeah, and I think the stories dictate the way the music should be. You don't want melodic things. It's percussive. It's surreal. Those little phrases he does really make it. There's a pizzicato thing he does that comes back again and again, and that's become a sort of signature. And some of the sustains. I think it's real art to use sustains and make them interesting, because if you sustain it through a long period and it doesn't have dynamics or whatever, it's boring. Sometimes you're not even aware of the music, which I think is really good; it puts you right into the picture. You never say, "Oh, I like that cue," because it's driving the story, which is what good music should do.

From a producer's perspective, what advice would you give musicians who aspire to do what Mark Snow is doing?

One thing I like about Mark is: Mark listens. He listens to me, he reads the scripts, he understands that he is in service to an idea, a show, and many other factors. And he does not try to overwhelm that. He knows he can't shout louder than the other voices. So what he's become is a wonderful collaborator. If I had to hire someone else, I'd hire someone who, like Mark, has talent to spare, but it's really about the work. It's not about the ego. It's about the music and the picture. What we do is we put pictures on screen with music, and he understands that. Once the two become separated, you're sunk. It all has to be a wonderful blend.

Looking into your crystal ball, do you foresee a day when the musical direction of this show might take a radical turn?

Maybe. It'll be dictated by the show. I know there's an upcoming episode where I want to use Khachaturian's "Saber Dance," very un-*X-Files*. And so if we drop that in there, Mark's going to have to figure out how to tailor what he does so this piece of music doesn't stand out like a sore thumb. We had an episode this year called "DPO," now known as "Lightning Boy," where we used rock songs. We used a Filter song, a Vandals song, and we used a James song, which actually was the inspiration for the whole show. And so, I think Mark had to find things in those songs to carry through the episode.

Are you surprised by the show's success?

No. But at the same time, I'm not blown away by it. Basically, all I want to do, and the other guys will tell you, is make sure there's a great show on each week.

[*Carter is summoned to the car waiting outside.*]

Final thoughts before you go?

Whenever I go to the conventions, and whenever I go online, people always have questions, comments, or huge compliments paid to Mark about the music. People realize that the music is a major part of this show's success, equal to many other parts: the writing, the producing, the acting, the photography, the art direction. All these things add up to make *The X-Files*. The music holds its own. It is of equal weight. God bless him. I'm going to do another project pretty soon, and I've already asked Mark to work on that with me because we've developed such a rapport.

What is that new project — can you say?

Sorry.

[*Note: The show in question was* Millennium.]

> **"The music is a major part of this show's success, equal to many other parts: the writing, the producing, the acting, the photography, the art direction. All these things add up to make The X-Files."**
> **—creator/producer Chris Carter**

act 3
composer MARK SNOW

Before diving into *The X-Files*, what TV work have you've done leading up to this show.

The longest running one I did before this, and it's an odd contrast to *The X-Files*, was *Hart to Hart*. That was with an orchestra, live players the whole way. Very traditional, very old-fashioned. I didn't know anything about Synclaviers or samplers back then.

And here you are today in the thick of technology, doing what might be the coolest, most cutting-edge show on the tube.

I'm so lucky. I've always wanted to have my own self-contained environment, with all the gear and all the stuff. To have the ultimate control has always been a dream of mine. My accountant, of all people, is responsible for me getting the Synclavier. These things are expensive, but at the time, I knew I had to get some type of home-studio situation going. It was a real stretch financially, but it's paid off big time. It's such an elegant piece of gear. Such a simplistic and clean-sounding system. It's fantastic. And quick, too. Instead of having keyboards all over the place, and patching and pulling and doing, it's instant. In fact, in this episode that you saw, there are a couple of fixes I have to make. And you can sit with me while I do it, and you can see how that works.

I noticed a few other noise-making items in your studio as well.

I just got into the Roland S-760, and that's a real cool adjunct to all the other MIDI gear I've got. It has a fabulous library, and I like the fact that it has a video screen.

When you first started doing *The X-Files*, was there ever any discussion about using an orchestra?

No. I think Chris Carter was looking for an out-there approach to the music, and luckily for me, Bob Goodwin recommended me to Chris. Chris came here and auditioned me in a very calm, cool way. In fact, he came back twice.

Did he give you any test cues to write?

No. He just came in, and I showed him some stuff from a project I was working on. It was enough for him to get a sense of the room, and a sense of my ideas, and so forth. Luckily it worked out. A big part of it, too, was the fact that he lived in Pacific Palisades, and he didn't want anybody who lived in the Valley.

When the green light was given, what conceptual overview did Chris give you?

The main thing he wanted to accomplish was he didn't want much, if any, emotional, melodic music. He basically wanted atmospheric, sustained, moody flavors. Since music is such an abstract, you say that kind of thing to one guy and he'll do his version of it, and so forth. Chris was very concerned that my concept of what he wanted was in line with his. So for the pilot, they took a bunch of music from all kinds of scores, and laid it in — a temp track.

What was your impression of the temp?

I was surprised by two things: There was a ton of music, and there were a lot of short cues with breaks. I thought one of those things would have to go. Either it would be fewer cues, but longer, or less total music. So what evolved from that was the first option: a lot of music — more than what would normally be used in a TV show. It has set the tone for this show in a unique way. I mean, there's sometimes upwards of 40 minutes of music, and the show is only 45 minutes long.

Chris seems to be a tough customer. He said he was very, very hands-on with you.

Early on, he was really on me, giving me all kinds of verbal instructions. My reaction to that, partly, was to be a little inhibited. You know, when somebody's on your case a lot — and it was very respectful, very constructive — it tends to make you a little gun-shy. "Yikes, I'd better get it just right." So I was a little inhibited during the first few shows, but then the thing started to grow. We found that we needed more accents. We needed bigger things. Just a constant drone wasn't going to be good enough. As the show evolved, and I started stretching it and moving it around, I got into some melodic stuff. But it was dark. It was gothic. It was moody. It was still in keeping with the show, but it stretched it more than the original idea. The original was sort of two-dimensional, and now it's more three-dimensional.

Once you had a few episodes under your belt, did you consider making any instrument templates, or stock motifs?

Well, we quickly found a group of sounds and instruments that were pleasing to everyone, and we just kept augmenting those. As I would get new gear or new sounds, I'd throw those in. I think nine times out of ten, he thought that was great. I mean, I've done every minute of music for every show so far — and I hope I'll be doing it till the end — but each show has its own sort of theme. Sometimes it's more cerebral and more thoughtful and introspective, and other times, like the show you just saw, it's this very big, physical epic with trains and planes and bombs, and the director is all over the place. It's outdoors. It's indoors. It's like a big feature. So all that has to be taken into account. And then when is the music sound design, and when is it music?

Backing up a second, you said you found a group of sounds that were pleasing to everyone. What were those?

I think in the beginning there was one thing I did that he just flipped for, and then we overused that a little bit. There was a sample I have of a huge string orchestra doing this random pizzicato sound. It starts out quiet and low, and gets louder and faster and higher in pitch. It's crazy and random, and it seems to work for many, many *X-File* scenes. Then there's another version of that. It's a live brass group that does the same thing. So you put that with a sustained thing, and it's very evocative.

Are these types of samples part of your Synclavier library?

Exactly. Also, there are special types of sustained sounds that have become staples of the show. There's a violin section sound that I've used in every show, in one way or another — either dissonant sustained or high, single-line, simple melodies. Another big musical staple of the show, if you will, is this pitch-bending sound that slides up or down. Sometimes that's either a single note, or a whole cluster of notes.

Is the bend part of the sample, or do you play those?

I play 'em with the . . . what do you call it, the mod wheel . . . the pitch wheel? [*Laughs.*] A little diversion here. My background is completely acoustic. I was an oboe player. I went to Juilliard. I was going to be a classical musician. This technical stuff, I know as much as I have to know. I can't compete with most of these guys who know the stuff. It's not that interesting to me. I just want something that will work really great, really quickly, and sound fantastic. I'll learn as much as I have to learn, but after that, it's more about the music.

Describe a typical *X-Files* week in the life of Mark Snow.

The first thing that'll happen is they'll send me a VHS rough-cut of the show, and I'll just view it to get a sense of what it's about. No note-taking, no nothing. Just watching. Then next the locked 3/4" [videotape] is sent to me along with the spotting notes from our music editor, Jeff Charbonneau. Jeff is fantastic. He's done many, many features. He's a very classy guy, and he's been on the show from day one. He's managed to get inside Chris's head in terms of knowing where music should go. So he spots the show completely by himself. In the beginning, we would spot it together, and it was kind of tedious because we were there with the sound effects guys, and it took forever and you really couldn't concentrate on one thing or the other. Now he does it by himself. He lives in the neighborhood, which is wonderful, and he sends me the notes. It's great. The joke about *The X-Files* spotting is: "Let's just spot where there isn't music," because it's practically wall-to-wall music.

What happens next?

I get the notes, and what I usually like to do is start with the biggest cue first: either the longest or most involved, which is usually in the last act.

What day of the week is this?

It changes. But let's just say, for example, over the weekend I've watched the rough cut. On Monday I get the 3/4" tape and the spotting notes, and I can start. I'll do the writing Monday, Tuesday, and Wednesday, and maybe a little bit on

Thursday. On Friday, they'll come over like they did today, and we mix it, send it out, and get ready for the next one.

During those three composing days, are you usually up all night, cranking away at the cues?

No. no. Absolutely not. I like the early hours. Businessman's hours. If I'm really pressed for time, I'll start early, like at around 7:00 or so in the morning, and go until the late afternoon or early evening. I like my nights to be free.

Let's zero in on a cue. You're watching the video, and I assume your music is entirely inspired by the visuals, as opposed to sifting through pre-made motifs and plugging them in.

Exactly. I'll go for that big fat cue first, and what that accomplishes is, if there's any kind of musical theme or sound theme, it can be established in that cue. And I know that's going to be the full gamut of the instruments and sounds. So after that's done, I'll have established my palette for the rest of the show. So it's that first cue that takes the longest, and is the hardest.

How precise do you try to get in terms of accenting visual actions with your music?

I'd say a majority of the music is supportive, sustaining-type sounds. One of the things Chris was very adamant about in the beginning was that there shouldn't be this Mickey Mouse approach: Somebody does something, somebody says a word, and "Bang!" That's an old-fashioned, very traditional approach, but I prefer to lay low and choose certain moments for crashing or bashing. That constant sustain and textural sound really got monotonous, so it was important that there were some really great crescendos and accents and percussion things to break up the din of that sustain. There are a lot of false starts in *The X-Files*. Scully and Mulder are sneaking around rooms, and they quickly make a turn, and there's nothing there. There's a lot of that. And the big accents always seem to work well there.

Are punches or streamers added to your video cut?

No. The Synclavier is synced to the video, but beyond that, no. I choose a tempo for the click, and I play along with it. Sometimes I don't use the click. Sometimes if I feel it needs something where the tempo isn't marked [*he sings, rigidly, "da-da-dadada"*] but more expressive, I'll just play along with it. I'll impro-

"One of the things Chris [Carter] was very adamant about in the beginning was that there shouldn't be this Mickey Mouse approach: Somebody says a word, and 'Bang!' That's an old-fashioned, very traditional approach, but I prefer to lay low and choose certain moments for crashing or bashing."
—Mark Snow

vise. Let's say I'm dealing with a five-minute cue that has three main sections: The first section is all talk, the next section is walking around with no dialog, and the third is a chase, capture, and smooth out. I'll approach each section separately at first, then connect them. I'll fill in the transitions so it will sound smooth — like one piece. What's happened is, I've turned into a first-rate improviser of film music.

[*Indeed he has. I watched Snow improvising a cue, and in two one-take passes, he had created a monster. On the first track he'd recorded various swells, accents, and crescendos, on the next he laid down a frantic, "Tarkus"-like left-hand piano motif.*]

Sometimes when I'm improvising, I'll fall upon something that is so great, I could never repeat it. Never. And hopefully, that red [record] light is on.

Do you sequence with the Macintosh?

Actually, no. The Synclavier is my sequencer. It's not this major high-powered sequencer, but it's just great for what I do.

Do you do much touch-up editing to your sequenced tracks?

Not too much. Occasionally I'll have a note that sounds wrong, and all I'll have to do is raise it a half-step, or lower it. But otherwise, not much.

If you're accenting an action with an orchestra hit or whatever, will you nudge the note around in the sequencer until it lines up just right?

No. I'll keep going back and forth live, real-time, until it's right.

Alf Clausen, composer of *The Simpsons*, talked about writing across bar lines. In other words, in film music, the time signature might be changing radically, but to the listener, the music just naturally flows. Do you find yourself thinking mathematically when you're composing for *The X-Files*?

God, no. Never. There's no sense of key, first of all. And there's definitely no sense of meter. Sometimes there will be a repetitive phrase that will have a sense of 3/4 or 4/4, but in general, it's this nebulous, free-flowing murk.

Your use of rhythmic motifs under action sequences is very effective. Do you typically build those patterns yourself, or lay in sampled loops?

They're usually played note-for-note. Once in a while I'll use a loop of African drumming or ethnic third-world stuff, and they're nice. You can fade them in and out, and even though they're rhythmic, they become sort of a sustained texture. If there's one really important thing about the music to this show, it's contrast. There are many long cues . . . ten-minute, eleven-minute, nine-minute, eight-minute cues. A lot of the time it's just people talking, and you have to sustain under it and support it. But you have to do something so it doesn't sound like wallpaper, like a din of noise. That's why things have to be added and subtracted, and percussion has to come in. That's what separates the good from the great when writing long cues. I mean, there are times when I add crescendos and accents that don't necessarily appear to be needed, but it heightens a line or a moment — even if there isn't some big, flailing, bashing fight or chase or something.

When you're watching a scene, and you've identified the feeling that you want to go for, do you think analytically at all? For example, "It's brooding, so minor chords would go nicely here." Do you play these types of mental games?

I do, but in big, broad strokes. I never get down to, "Hmm, a major second or a suspended ninth. . . ." Nothing like that. Let's say mystery or sneaking around or brooding or darkness, then that certainly evokes "pathy" music. Very connected. Very gooey. Lugubrious-type sustained things. And I'll definitely focus into that group. But then I'm always looking for that place where you can perk it up with some other color. The worst thing about electronic music or home studio music is the color and the dynamics come out sounding so limited.

Mark Snow on "The X-Files *sound*": "There's no sense of key, first of all. And there's definitely no sense of meter. Sometimes there will be a repetitive phrase that will have a sense of 3/4 or 4/4, but in general, it's this nebulous, free-flowing murk.

Shifting gears for a moment, what happens if you get sick? Do you have a sub who can come in and do the gig for you in a pinch?

Well, luckily, that hasn't happened. I've been sick, but, I could always drag myself out to the studio and do it. But failing that, there are hours of continuous music I've written [for past episodes] that could be pieced together.

Who would be responsible for selecting the material and laying it in?

The music editor, Jeff Charbonneau. He'd probably sit with Chris and go through it. There's so much material to draw from, they could probably get the job done without too much trouble.

Have you ever been stumped — writer's block?

No, but the hardest part is the beginning. Coming up with the right combinations of sounds for a particular piece. Sometimes it's abstract, and if you ask me why I chose that sound or that instrument, it would be difficult to explain. It just felt right.

What's the story of writing the theme song?

It's a fun story. Chris Carter, at the beginning, was inundating me with all kinds of music, from the Smiths and Portishead to Philip Glass and Steve Reich. Third-world stuff, you name it. And I did, I'd say, five different passes based on our conversations. Chris was very patient and very encouraging, but every time he'd say, "That's great, but what if we. . . ." And again, and again.

What did those earlier versions sound like?

They were a lot more conventional, perhaps. Not really melodic.

Did any have a drum groove under them?

"If there's one really important thing about the music to this show, it's contrast. There are many long cues . . . ten-minute, eleven-minute, nine-minute, eight-minute cues. A lot of the time it's just people talking, and you have to sustain under it and support it. But you have to do something so it doesn't sound like wallpaper, like a din of noise. That's why things have to be added and subtracted, and percussion has to come in. That's what separates the good from the great when writing long cues."
—Mark Snow

Some, yes, but never a drum set. There were percussion things, but there was never any sense of pop or rock. But finally I felt comfortable enough with him to say, "We're getting close, but let's try something. Let me just go off on my own and completely clear my head of everything we've talked about, and everything I've done, and see what I can come up with." Chris respected me enough, thank goodness, to go for it. So, what happened was, I accidentally had one of these delay/echo units on, and I played the triplet figure. And the thing kept repeating. And I thought, "That's pretty good. That's not a real heavy rhythm, but it's an evocative sound. Okay, if I put a sustain combination over that, what's that like? Interesting. Okay. Now, it needs one final element." Which was the melody.

So I tried it on various instruments: violins, flutes, woodwinds, brass, voices, and combinations of all those things. But they were all too damn ordinary.

So I tried some ethnic instruments. Too much. Too busy. Not distinctive enough. So, on my [E-mu] Proteus/2, there was this whistle. I thought, "Nah, that's too silly. But, okay, try it." I started fiddling around with it, and it started to happen.

My wife was walking around, she heard it, and she jumped in and said, "You know, that is cool. It's different. It's unique." And then Chris heard it.

What did he say?

Much to his credit, because it's kind of a stretch on this show, he liked it. And the more he heard it, the more he liked it. I'll never forget, though, there was a meeting of executives, producers, and writers, and I played it for them.

What happened?

They all sat there, staring at each other. And it was, at best, a very cool reception to it. But the same thing happened. The more they heard it . . . it just started to develop a life of its own. Now it's been nominated for an Emmy, and the response has been overwhelming.

act 4
sound supervisor THIERRY J. COUTURIER

Define your role on *The X-Files*.

As the sound supervisor, I'm involved in the overall sound design and the sound quality of the show. I get the show after it's been edited and the picture is locked. At that point I sit with the producers and we go through and talk about production sound problems, ADR, and what kind of sounds, backgrounds, and effects we want to hear. The typical sounds of guns and backgrounds and stuff are pretty obvious, but of course on *The X-Files* there are so many odd things, aliens or strange people or. . . . So after we discuss the obvious elements, I'll hand the show off to the dialog editors who work on cleaning up the dialog. I'll break the show down, program the ADR, and send cue sheets up to the actors in Vancouver and the rest to the actors in L.A.

Explain ADR.

ADR, Automated Dialog Replacement, is when we replace lines of dialog that need to be redone because the production sound quality was noisy or bad, or when there are added scripted lines.

Does that type of replacement have to be done often?

Not as much as in the beginning. This is a very hard show to do, technically, because they're on location a lot or they're using big wind machines or have production effects happening. Our production sound mixer, Michael Williamson, has been getting better and better at trying to get the dialog as clean as possible under these circumstances.

Who else do you interact with?

There are effects editors who cut the backgrounds and effects, and there's a Foley team: two Foley walkers and a Foley mixer. We completely Foley the whole show.

Do you primarily use live acoustic Foley, or do you also use samples?

Well, a lot of the backgrounds come from material that's shot live or from libraries. The company I work for is West Productions, and Dave West has accumulated a library of tens of thousands of effects that he's recorded or created over the years. The editors also bring in materials that they've acquired or created. So we draw from existing libraried material, and when we need to, we create or shoot new things.

What format are the effects stored in?

A lot of material is on DATs, 1/4" tape, and CDs. Some effects were originally shot onto Beta hi-fi, but that's all been transferred to other formats. We haven't brought in any CD-ROM libraries yet, but we will.

Once you pick a sound to use, how do you drop it into the soundtrack?

We use a 24-track and the [Tascam] DA-88s to get our effects to the stage. To edit the hard effects we use a WaveFrame system, which is, in effect, our sampler. When sound effects are cut on a frame, you don't usually trigger it from a keyboard, you actually find the place where it starts, you can see it on the screen, and you cut it right there, play it back, manipulate it, and so forth. Then that material is either dumped to DA-88 or onto a 24-track. The dialog is cut on one of the WaveFrame systems, and that stays in the digital domain. The ADR is also shot directly into and edited in the WaveFrame. The ADR and dialog then get put on WaveFrame hard drives on the dubbing stage.

What's the craziest or most challenging thing you've done to get a sound?

The Gimlet was a sound we were trying to get where an alien knife-like device slides out of a little metal tube and gets stuck in the back of these duplicate aliens who then deflate and turn to mush. So, "What is that sound?" And everyone had a different concept. It came down to, "Make it sound like a silencer." So we got a couple of silencers, but it still wasn't right. So finally Paul [Rabwin] said, "Does it sound like this?" [*Vocalizes a white-noise sound burst: "pfffft."*] "Yeah, that's it." So we shot that in the mic, sucking in and out, and that was it. And that was, literally, six hours of time over a three-day period to get to that effect. Another complex one were these wingless mites that would fly and swarm and attack and kill people. That ended up being. . . . We'd go through bunches of tracks to get each to sound right. It had to be bee-like, and fly-like, it had to have movement, it was electronic, it was humming, it was this, it was that. We kept coming up with different groups of sounds, combinations of pitched organic sounds — some played backward, some pitched, mixed with some locusts and wasps and flies buzzing in a jar — and finally we had enough to cut through Mark's goddamn score. [*Laughs.*]

How much time do you typically have to prepare an episode?

Usually we have between four and eight days. The normal turnaround if we get a show on Monday is to dub [mix] it the following Tuesday.

Describe the dubbing process.

After everything is assembled and Mark sends over the music, we go to the stage with separate music tracks, Foley tracks, background tracks, effects tracks, ADR tracks, and dialog tracks. Dave West, Nello Torri, and Doug Turner mix the show. I can't tell you how much of the wonderful and original nature of our dub was and is created by our mixers. We used to have two days to dub the show, but we went into overtime so much, we decided this year to go to three days. It's given us the luxury of having the time to see how all the sounds and backgrounds and effects are going to marry with the music, because this show has *so* much music in it. A typical show has an average of 12 minutes of music for a one-hour show, or 24 minutes for a two-hour movie. *The X-Files* averages 38 minutes for a one-hour show! And the nature of the music eats up so much of the midrange, it fills up so much sound, that we often have to work sound effects around it. The battle becomes: "What do we really want to hear? How much of this? How much of that? What's not important?" Chris Carter is usually the happiest when the sound effects feel like they're part of the music. From time to time we hear viewers complain about how loud the music is, but what we've tried to do is push the TV sound envelope as far as it will go.

How many tracks are you usually dealing with?

On average, anywhere from 65 to 90 tracks. Generally we keep the dialog down to, maybe, seven tracks; we try to keep the ADR down to eight tracks, but it can go as high as 14 or 16 when we need it; the effects take between 24 and 32 tracks, more, again, if we need it; and the music will usually come in four to six stereo pairs.

Do you use Surround Sound?

This year we've gone to Dolby four-track Surround Sound, which has given us more room in the mix. It's allowed us to separate things more: left, right, center, surround. Then, when it collapses to two-track stereo, it actually holds up a bit better. In other words, loud, but clear.

Mark Snow's music is very dynamic. Do you ever worry about sending out signals that might fry the average TV speaker?

Sometimes we play back on Auratones to see what the average TV speaker reception will sound like, but what happens on the air, in any case, is when the network sends the signal to the satellite, they chop off everything below 200Hz and everything above 12.5kHz. So the dynamics Mark creates are often diminished by the nature of the broadcast signal. They literally lop off the bottom and top end, which takes out some of the nuances in his music and the dynamics of our dub. When you hear it off the air, you can't think about that. It is what it is. But if you hear it here in the studio, it's, "God, there's so much range." If you have your TV connected to your stereo, you can hear a tremendous amount of dynamics that you don't hear off a 3" television speaker. But the overall level and balance still translates relatively well to regular TVs.

act 5
music editor JEFF CHARBONNEAU

How did you get involved in doing the temp score for *The X-Files*?

The studio called me and told me to come over and meet Chris Carter, who needed a temporary score for his pilot. So I met with him and went through and found a style of music he was comfortable with, which was fairly electronic and non-melodic. He wanted to create a soundscape that was sort of based on minimalist music. So I helped him with that, and we ended up with a lot of electronic sounds. He liked electronic music, but he didn't like "standard" synthesizer sounds, so we found some interesting textures and put together a temporary score.

In other words, the temp was a collage of pre-existing music.

Exactly. It was just an example to sell the idea to the network, and most network people can't sit through most temps without hearing the music and some sort of effects track, and for good reason. I've been doing this on feature films for some time; I come in before the composers and put together temporary scores.

That, of course, evolved into a full-time gig on this show. What are your responsibilities as music editor during a typical production cycle?

What we've established is a little different from traditional shows in that I spot the show alone, after which I confer with Mark, and then we present our notes to the producers. If they have any changes, they call up and say, "We think there should be music in this scene and that scene, but not here," and so on. And, "We want you to specifically accent this action." We don't have a lot of time for each episode, and Mark's an amazingly fast writer. He can sit down and sketch out a ten-minute piece in a day, which is pretty prolific for most composers. From that point, if there's any other music that needs to be put in, say, a song or source music, I'll then start working on that. We had an episode earlier this season called "DPO" in which we used a lot of [pre-produced] songs, and they needed to be edited to match action. So I'll edit those, and put 'em on video and I'll give them to the producers. They might say, "We need something here, a snare roll, maybe," and I'll add those things. From that point, Mark writes the score, and he auditions it for the producers, which I try to stay away from, and that seems to have worked out really well. Generally there are minimal changes at that session. Then he and Larold [Rebhun, mix-meister] put it on DA-88 tape. I get the tape, load it into my editing system, a Fostex Foundation, go through and quality-check it, and that goes onto an MO [magneto-optical] drive. I also back it up to DAT, so we have multiple versions of it. From there it goes to the dubbing stage.

Do you ever have to make any last-second changes or additions at the dubbing stage?

Sometimes they'll ask me to fill in holes, or punctuate something. I have a semi-compatible library with Mark's, and I use an [E-mu] EIV and a [Yamaha] VL1 to program similar types of effects, and add those. Sometimes I'll take some of Mark's existing music and stretch it or compress it, and make it work in scenes where there is no music — things like that. They might ask for an ambient-type drone or some other type of musical effect at the last minute. Most of the time it works out pretty well.

It must be nice to not have to deal with reams of manuscript paper on this gig. In fact, you guys don't deal with any notation.

Pretty much, yeah, that's true. We've notated only one thing, and that was the main title — and that was for the Emmys. They needed it for the band, which is funny to me: How do you interpret a digital delay sound for the left hand?

act 6
mixer LAROLD REBHUN

You've been slaving away at the mixing desk all afternoon. What are your official job duties?

I'm the scoring mixer. The only main music I don't mix is if there's a source . . . like a band who has a record, they just send it in and Jeff Charbonneau takes it. I've known Mark for about five years, and I mix most of the stuff he does. He writes to the picture, and puts all the dynamics into the Synclavier, so my job is just getting a balance, and making sure it gets on tape okay. And making sure it sounds good.

Then once you've signed off, the dubbing engineers get their hands on it, right?

Yeah. At the dubbing session there are three guys. One does the dialog, one does the sound effects, and one guy does the music, and they all make sure everything can be heard. They know what they're doing, and they know what it takes, but sometimes it's a drag when you hear this beautiful music and there's all these helicopters and stuff on top of it. You can't really hear it on the air, and that's why a lot of folks have been asking about Mark's CD.

Although the Synclavier seems to be Mark's main instrument, he has a bunch of MIDI modules as well. What percentage of sounds usually come from the Synclav versus the MIDI rack?

Mark gets into these modes that change over the course of a couple of months. He just got a new Roland sampler [S-760], so now he's got three stereo pairs coming out of that. But from my point of view, all of those six sounds come up on one stereo pair of faders. Today we probably had 14 to 16 Synclavier tracks working, the piano is from an outboard module [Kurzweil MicroPiano], that's a stereo pair, there's a low-end thing which is a Proteus/2, and the Roland. That's pretty much it today. So it was probably ten tracks of outboard stuff and 14 to 16 tracks of Synclavier.

A lot of *The X-Files* music is very ambient. On the right is Mark's effects rack. Do you handle a lot of the effects work?

Yeah, but Mark does a lot of tweaking internally in the Synclavier. So I don't really add very many effects except the reverb. I usually use four effects. I have a really short room which works well on some individual synthy-sounding things. It sounds like a room about 30 x 30 feet. Then I have a longer reverb, and then a really long reverb for super-effecty stuff. Like, today he had those marcato strings going [*sings: "dodo-DO-dododo"*], and a long reverb wouldn't work on that, so I had to dial that back. And then I have a really quick stereo delay for violins, which are mono Synclavier samples. I just turn that up a little bit and it spreads 'em out in stereo — makes it a little wider. Otherwise you've got these stereo sounds, and a single mono violin. It doesn't really blend like a real orchestra should. Those are the only effects I really use.

Were you involved in Mark's happy delay accident when he was writing the theme song?

No [*laughs*]. In fact, when I was mixing the main title for the first time, I just didn't get it. It was just weird to me; it took several months before I went, "Oh yeah, that's pretty cool." It was an odd thing. I remixed it for the third season, and sonically it's better, but it's different because the show's now in Surround Sound. I put some stereo delays on there, as opposed to the old mono delay, and I think the Dolby Surround plays with the level of the delays.

Is Mark's studio equipped to deal with Surround Sound settings?

They take this stereo mix that we do on the DA-88, and they pipe it through their matrix. Here, I just didn't have the cables or the speakers to stick it up in the back. But the guys at the dubbing stage really wanted me to monitor through it. I'm trying to be real careful as far as what's out of phase, and things like that. But occasionally Mark comes up with some sound that I know is out of phase, but if he's got a couple of other sounds that are similar, I'll just stick that in there also so there will be something that kind of goes around the room. Sometimes I get complaints from the dubbing guys: "Too much stuff in the Surrounds." But for the people who have the Surround Sound systems, it's a little something extra for them.

How different is it to mix a TV cue compared to mixing a pop/rock tune?

Well, speed, for one thing. I mean, I can mix this show in three or four hours. Doing rock and roll records, you mix a song a day, or whatever. I have friends who just can't believe how fast this thing goes. A lot of it has to do with the equipment, and a lot of it has to do with Mark and I knowing each other by now. When we first started working together, I had to put new tape down and re-label the board for every cue. I had to get different EQ. . . . It just took forever. Now he writes in groups, so he'll tell me, "These four cues use the similar sounds," so I'll do those. Then I'll switch over to another set. Other than that, I'm mixing this as if it's going to be on a CD eventually.

*[by Greg Rule, **Keyboard**, March 1996]*

n.e.d.
synclavier

*i*n the 1980s, the Synclavier was a beast of mythical proportions. Carrying an initial price tag in the area of $500,000, a fully-equipped Synclavier system was so far beyond the financial means of even relatively successful musicians that its attributes took on a mystic aspect. The impression was that mere mortals could not understand its capabilities, much less its operation. Add to this a decidedly serpentine developmental history: The instrument began as the first commercially available digital keyboard synthesizer, sprouted a video screen shortly thereafter, and metamorphosed into one of the first major sampling instruments. Such abrupt shifts in the Synclavier's commercial identity served to push the instrument farther into the murky recesses of high-end mystery. None of that, it seemed, was intentional

vital stats

Description: The first commercially available digital keyboard synthesizer, but it sprouted a video screen shortly thereafter, and metamorphosed into one of the first major sampling and hard disk recording instruments.

Manufacturer: New England Digital, White River Junction, Vermont.

Original Price: approximately $500,000.

on the part of the Synclavier's manufacturer, a small Vermont company called New England Digital.

Picking up where a Dartmouth College research project left off in 1973, founders Cameron Jones and Sydney Alonso, along with musical consultant Jon Appleton, simply began to work out the implications of their investigations into the technology of digital synthesis. As N.E.D.'s president, a tall, enthusiastic Berklee-schooled former percussionist named Brad Naples, stated, "The Synclavier had to go through the process of evolution; that was one of the strongest points of the whole system. It was a continuously evolving process. N.E.D.'s approach was to incorporate functions that musicians usually associate with several separate pieces of equipment . . . the notion that keyboard control, digital sound generation, and sampling capability ought to reside in a single box. This is the order in which the Synclavier originally developed.

"We were a computer manufacturer," Naples stressed. "That was always the problem with people's image of N.E.D. They thought it was a synthesizer company, which was absolutely, totally wrong. It was always a computer manufacturer that happened to pick its niche in the music industry."

The keyboard unit was always the Synclavier's most prominent feature. In addition to the velocity- and pressure-sensing keyboard, pitchbend, and modulation wheels, the Synclav's case housed a simple front panel consisting of an

LED display, several banks of red buttons, and a data-entry knob. Software determined the functions of the buttons, so the same front panel served the instrument through many revisions in overall capability. The computer handled the details of these functions via a Terminal Support Option, as well as the system's constellation of software-driven features, such as the Timbre Display System (synthesizer voicing), Script (the sequencing language), a scoring and notation program, polyphonic sampling, the Signal File Manager (for analyzing and editing sampled waveforms), resynthesis, and SMPTE capabilities. Hardware options were available as well, such as extra synthesizer voices and additional storage.

Long before the advent of Digidesign's Pro Tools software, Naples' foresaw the Synclavier as "the recording studio of the future. You don't need that big console. You don't need that tape machine or all those musicians. We feel that the whole audio production process is going to be computerized, and we want to be involved in that. We want to be involved in reducing the amount of knobs and EQ settings you have to turn, in reducing your razor blade stock, in reducing the number of egotistical musicians you have to hire. If you hire a major orchestra it's running you $8,000 an hour, and all you want to do is put down a string line."

[by Ted Greenwald, Keyboard, April 1986]

depeche mode

Electronica for the Masses

What is the appeal of Depeche Mode? They don't rakishly sling guitars waist-high. They don't moonwalk or crotch-grab. They don't even dress that spectacularly; moody, art-student black seems to be their motif. That leaves us with the music. (A band known mainly for its music? What a concept.) But the mystery remains. Though originally an upbeat, hand-clappy, proto-synth rock band, Depeche Mode has cultivated a sound that manages to be both depressing and catchy ever since Vince Clarke bailed out from the group to start Erasure. It's not dance music, especially when measured against records currently lumped into that category. It's not large-scale, ambitious, arty stuff. Neither is it commercial; after 11 years, their sound remains as paradoxical as ever — paradoxical because, despite all the muffled drums, the peculiar combinations of percussion sounds in their drum tracks, the groaning vocals, alternately menacing and vaguely bored, Depeche Mode strikes a chord.

Maybe their endurance has something to do with it. Long after many other pioneering synth rock groups sequenced their last synth bleeps, the Mode is still at it. From their first post-Clarke project, *Broken Frame*, through the release of *Songs of Faith and Devotion*, they've devoted ample time to perfecting whatever it is that defines their style. With U2's longtime producer, Flood, presiding, the *Songs* sessions added up to eight months of meticulous recording, mixing, and

Depeche Mode, the *Ultra* era: Martin Gore, Dave Gahon, Andrew Fletcher (left to right).

◄·····················

tweaking. As a result, we have an album on which their sound is — paradox again — more developed yet more enigmatic than ever.

For which producer Flood can take a lot of credit. His main clients, the guys in U2, seem to have melted under his direction into a single blob-like noise, from which chiming guitars and desperate singing only occasionally escape. So it is on *Songs*: You can pick out most of the parts, but the mix encourages you to absorb the music as a whole. "This is the dawning of our love," the key line on the first single, "I Feel You," comes at you as part of a welter of throbbing bass, crashing cymbals, ear-piercing guitar overtones, and squealing general electronica. But while details may have been clearer on some of their previous releases, the sound is still unmistakably theirs.

The crucial element in this sound is Alan Wilder, unabashedly identified in the band's PR as their "musician." Wilder spent more time with Flood than his colleagues doing what he calls the "screwdriver" work. Shortly before flying back to England to rehearse for their tour, he took time out to reflect on *Songs* and ponder the enduring enigma of Depeche Mode.

Do you feel that in terms of sound, *Songs of Faith and Devotion* differs from previous Depeche Mode albums?

It certainly does represent something quite different, which was our objective. We wanted to try and change as many things about our approach to making music as we possibly could, mainly to keep ourselves interested in what we're doing and to challenge ourselves. We were very aware of getting caught in easy routines and becoming bored. I suppose the emphasis is much more on performing on this record. But once that performance was created, we applied all the technology we've come to know and love over the years to put it together in a way that's still uniquely Depeche Mode.

In what respect does performance play a bigger role than usual? Are you sequencing fewer parts?

We still sequence quite a lot of the performance, but we're using the sequencer to restructure what we do. When we just go in and play together, we end up sounding like a pub rock band. That's the problem: We're not capable of going into a room, playing together, and coming up with some magical piece of music. We have to apply all that technology to make it sound more spontaneous and human. One of the things I felt before we started this record was that the last album, good as it was, had a slight rigidity. We wanted to make this record much looser, less programmed. I think we achieved that objective.

What's an example of how the performance element comes through on _Songs_?

Let's take "I Feel You." All the drums on there are played. Most of them were sampled and then sequenced in the form of drum loops. That's not to say that they don't change as the song goes on. There's a series of loops, which are sequenced together, using [Steinberg] Cubase, in a different structure from how they were originally performed.

In the past, you might have programmed the rhythm without any performance.

Exactly. In this case, we're applying the technology to a performance to make sure that you get all the dynamics of a human performance, all those slight timing changes that make something feel human. On "Walking in My Shoes," for example, there are different loops in the verse, an additional loop comes in on the bridge, and the chorus brings in a complete change of drum sound and rhythm. Plus there are different drum fills, hi-hat patterns, and top percussion parts in each section. The combination of all that gives you the impression of the rhythm changing all the time.

To my ears, many of the parts played by the band sound more obscured on this record than on previous Depeche Mode albums.

Perhaps, to a degree. I would like to think that there's enough clarity within the sound that you can pick out the parts. But I suppose you should always go for a blend. That's what you try to create with your mix. A good mix should stop you from thinking about the mix. If you start analyzing all the details within a mix, you're not really experiencing the music as a whole. To get specific about it, people sometimes mix drums too loudly. Certainly, a lot of dance music is very rhythm-oriented. We place a lot of importance on rhythm as well, but sometimes loud drums aren't warranted. It can be very hard to mix drums quietly, because we're all brainwashed into hearing them right up front. As soon as you mix them quietly, you think it must be wrong.

The changes in the rhythm patterns and the placement of the drums in the mix on "In Your Room" were the most dynamic element in that song.

That song was quite difficult. We recorded the song three or four different ways. One was entirely as you hear it in the second verse, with the smaller drum kit and the "groovy" bass line. But the whole song with that rhythm wasn't strong enough; it didn't go anywhere. We had the song structure from a fairly early stage. We knew where we wanted the verses, choruses, and middle eights. So much as I did with "I Feel You," I went in and played drums along with the track in one particular style, then did it again in a funkier style, and so on.

The drum sounds themselves seemed to change from one section to the next.

We recorded those drums at a villa we had rented in Madrid. We set up a studio in the basement. The two drum kits, the smaller one and the larger one, were recorded in different spaces, which gave each a different kind of edge. Plus they were played in very different ways. The smaller drum kit, which comes in during the second verse, has quite an interesting loop going around it; it's another drum kit that's reduced by being put through a synthesizer and then distorted. That turns it into weird percussion sound, which is then looped to offset against the real drums and form an unusually funky groove. We often do things like that. We'll record a drum kit fairly straightforwardly, balance it together, and put the whole thing through a synthesizer. At the beginning of "I Feel You," for example, the drum kit is played, sampled, put through a synth, distorted, and then reduced to half-level.

What kind of synth would you typically use on drum sounds?

It could be anything. We've used a Roland 700 modular system. We've also used distortion boxes, filter sections. Often we use guitar effects processors. We're quite fond of the Zoom; it has great distortion and compression effects.

At the height of the crescendo in "In Your Room," we get the line, "Your eyes cause flames to arise." That's the one part of the album where you underscored a single word, with a cymbal roll behind "flames."

That was a late addition. Since that's such an up part of the song, it felt necessary to add something at that point. We put it in at the mix. It's often not un-

JAY BLAKESBERG

til you get to the mix stage that it becomes obvious that another part is required. When you're in the recording process, you've never got it sounding good enough to tell. So quite a few of those embellishments get put on at the mix stage, like backwards cymbals.

What attracts you to reversed sounds? There are plenty of them on this record, and on previous Depeche Mode albums too.

I'm not quite sure, but I'm nearly always the one who suggests those sounds, so it must have something to do with me. I suppose it's the strange psychedelic effect. Having taken psychedelic drugs in my youth, it reminds me of listening to music in that state of mind: Everything sounds backwards. So when I hear something backwards, it takes me off into a sort of trippy mood. You can also use backwards sounds to lead from one section to another, or form weird fills from a verse into a chorus.

There's a backwards episode at the end of "Mercy."

Dave Gahon's personal struggles almost spelled the end of Depeche Mode in the mid-'90s, but to many a Modehead's surprise, he and the band came back stronger than ever.

That's a backwards high piano. And the beginning of "Judas" has Uillean pipes recorded straight, with backwards reverb mixed in. The nice thing about backwards reverb is that it adds space to a sound without making it washy. I'm against using a lot of reverb most of the time, because I can't stand the distancing effect it makes. But I do often want to hear sounds in a space, or try to keep all the clarity of a sound while still trying to put it somewhere. Backwards reverb can do exactly that. There's a part in the middle of "Rush," the sort of progressive rock track near the end of the album, where the voice has lots of backwards reverb; that really sets the vocal part off.

Do you also subject your piano sounds to a lot of processing?

Quite often we do. The piano part at the beginning of "Walking in My Shoes" was put through a guitar processor, which distorted it and made it more edgy. We added a harpsichord sample on top of that. And on "Condemnation," we put the piano through some kind of a wobbly pitch-shifter. The idea of that track was to enhance the gospel feel that the song originally had without going into pastiche, and to try to create the effect of it being played in a room, in a space. So we began by getting all four members of the group to do one thing each in the same space. Fletcher was bashing a flight case with a pole, Flood and Dave were clapping, I was playing a drum, and Martin was playing an organ. We listened back to it. It was embryonic, but it gave us an idea for a direction.

There's a lot of guitar on this album, but it's never played in a clichéd, blues/metal style. It seems as if the kinds of samples and synth sounds you use dictate just how you can use it.

We have a very strong aversion to typical rock guitar playing. Something has to be said about the intensity that rock records have, but we would like to recreate that intensity in our own way, without resorting to those tactics. The idea of a high, screaming guitar part might translate into radio frequency waves, for example. Our guitar parts, on the other hand, tend to go quite weird. We run them through Leslies and other devices that make them less and less guitar-like while still keeping some of the power of the instrument.

Have you added much new equipment since the last album?

Not really. The only change is that we're using more acoustic instruments, especially for writing. When we're working out songs together, we usually play guitar, piano, bass, and drums. They're the most fun instruments to play, really. Each one is so dynamically pleasing. The only problem is that the sound of the piano can sometimes dictate what you write. It seems to be helpful to compose on instruments that give you lots of dynamic response. But then we'll transfer what we've written to a sound that's completely different, and the riff takes on a new quality.

Your electronic setup hasn't changed much in recent years?

We've still got the same selection of samplers — Akais and [E-mu] Emulators. And lots of rackmounted and modular synths: a Minimoog, Oberheims, the Roland 700 system, ARP 2600s. There are fewer modern synthesizers than ever before — no DX7s, PPGs, or things like that.

Is it a question of sound or limited programmability that steers you away from newer gear?

It's sound. If we felt that the DX7 had great sounds, we'd use it all the time. The older synthesizers have an organic quality, a roundness and grittiness, that you just don't hear on digital things. But the flexibility is important too. You've got so much flexibility of routing the sound on the older gear; you can create your own patches without adapting somebody's factory sample. The DX7 did initially impress me, because it had bell-like sounds that weren't readily available at that time. But you were fucked if you wanted to change those sounds, unless you had a very thorough understanding of algorithms. Nobody I know could get their head 'round that. I certainly couldn't.

As a member of Depeche Mode, you've got an inside perspective in assessing the impact of electronic technology on pop music over this past decade. How do you feel about how bands typically use this equipment?

I'm mainly disappointed. It's a shame to see electronics really being utilized only in the dance area. But, you know, though we're cited as being so instrumental in developing electronic dance music, we're trying to move as far away from that as we can. That's purely because the emphasis of what we do is on songs.

"It's a shame to see electronics really being utilized only in the dance area. But, you know, though we're cited as being so instrumental in developing electronic dance music, we're trying to move as far away from that as we can. That's purely because the emphasis of what we do is on songs." **—Alan Wilder**

Everything has to enhance the song, to create the right atmosphere. I do love dance music and Kraftwerk and techno; you're always going to see that side of us come through. But you've got to apply it to the song. And sometimes rigid electronics don't apply to songs that are more warm and emotional.

What do you think about changing tastes in synthesizer sound?

There's good and bad. A lot of people in rap music are using the technology in an interesting way to make their records sound dirty. So much of pop music is so clean and pristine, and there's an awful lot of bollocks because of it. I like to try and capture both sounds, to make it clear, with a full frequency range across the board, but also to have a lot of grit. Take "Mercy," for example. We were going for this rap-like drum loop. If you listen to that track with just the rhythm and one or two other elements going, it sounds fuckin' great. You can whack out all kinds of low-end distortion on the bass drum. But as soon as you start introducing other instruments over the top, it begins to sound wooly and waffly down in the low end, and you've got to start compromising your rhythm sounds in order to fit on all the other parts. As soon as you do that, you can start to lose all the drive. That was really a difficult song to mix.

Do you intentionally use low-bit samplers to maintain a grunge element in your sounds?

There's definitely something to be said for that. The first Emulator sounds great because it's such a bad quality. It's the same with analog tape; that hiss can be brilliant.

What sampler do you use for your drum sounds?

Generally the Akai S1100, not so much for its sound quality, which is fine, but because it triggers much tighter than the Emulator. And the way it assigns outputs has so many advantages over the Emulator, although I think the sound of the Emulator is slightly better.

What keyboard will you be using onstage for the tour?

Possibly the [E-mu] Emaxes, because they're convenient and roadworthy. It would be useful to have something that has an extra octave on it, though, because we have to assign so many sounds across the keyboard for each song.

Will you carry any extra musicians?

Possibly, perhaps singers. All I know is that I'm going to be playing some live drums, and Martin will almost certainly be playing more guitar. I suppose we'll be leaning more toward being a "rock band," but I certainly hope we won't be creating that general effect.

[by Robert L. Doershuk, **Keyboard, May 1993]**

Fast-forward to 1997. It was an action-packed year for Depeche Mode — now a three-man group. The departure of keyboardist Alan Wilder in 1995, coupled with frontman David Gahon's near-death antics a year later, almost drove a stake through the heart of Depeche Mode. But to many a Modehead's amazement, the remaining members (Gore, Fletcher, and Gahon) managed to pick up the pieces and carry on.

Ultra (Mute Records) was Depeche Mode's 12th full-length release, and while down-tempo was the name of the game (the swiftest track topped out at a turtle-like 100 bpm), the CD turned out to be an ear magnet. "Barrel of a Gun," the first track out of the gate, was one of the most riveting Mode singles to date — replete with throbbing synths, liquid bass, slappy percussion, sci-fi bleeps, and tortured vocals. And there was plenty more where that came from.

The subsequent singles, "It's No Good," "Home," and "Useless," all received substantial airplay.

With Tim Simenon (Bomb The Bass) and his production team in tow, the band locked themselves into the studio and emerged 15 months later with a remarkable new record. When Simenon got the call to produce *Ultra*, he came loaded . . . with ideas and people, that is. Dave Clayton was one of Simenon's synth men on the project, and he brought a fat track-record of onstage and studio experience, having worked with the likes of ABC, Bob Marley, George Michael, Take That, and U2. Needless to say, he was an obvious target for our interview microphone.

"Initially I got a demo tape from Martin [Gore]," said Clayton, of his early involvement in the *Ultra* project. "It was a pretty basic format — the essence of the songs was there — but he gave us rough pointers of where to go. So we started assembling the songs from there." Clayton and Kerry Hopwood handled keyboard and drum programming work, respectively.

Using "Barrel of a Gun" as an example, Clayton explained the process: "That one started off with a very strong melody, and the lyrics were there. He [Gore] had a little loop on the demo, a bass, a pad, and couple of the guitar lines. It was very sparse. Even though we basically started over from scratch, we tried not to lose the essence of the demo."

Using Gore's tape as a guide, the team began rebuilding the song from the bottom up. The infectious drum pattern was "a combination of a cut-up loop," explained Clayton, "just the top end of it, and single shots of bass drum, snare, and so forth. It wasn't a loop, *per se*. It was a pattern, but I think it had the feel of a loop."

Sequencing was done on "an old Atari with Notator. I've tried everything else, but the ST seems to have the best feel." The signature space warbles came from a combination patch made on a Waldorf Wave, and a Korg Trinity Plus and M1R. "A lot of people think it's just a preset synth," he said of the latter, "but once you get into it, there's a lot to be had."

The slippery "Barrel" bass line was recorded on a PPG Wave 2.3, but when the synth took a nose-dive a few weeks into the session, and prior to printing the keyboard parts to tape, Clayton feared the patch was lost forever. "Fortunately, I got it back, but it gave me quite a scare." Other synths exhumed from Clayton's vault for the sessions were an EMS Synthi, Oberheim Four-Voice, ARP 2600, and Roland JD-800 and Jupiter-8.

Reflecting back on the project, Clayton claimed that "it wasn't just like another keyboard session for me, at all. Even though I was brought in as a session man, I was given loads of freedom. For days and days I'd sit at my rig and experiment. They gave me a few pointers, but the overall attitude was, 'Hey, do whatever the hell you feel.' So I switched the stuff on and created like mad."

I also rolled tape with songwriter Martin Gore after *Ultra's* release, and was able to fire off a dozen questions in the allotted time; appropriate, perhaps, since *Ultra* was the band's 12th album.

When Alan left the band, did it feel like the end?

As bad as things were, I don't think any of us felt that we wanted to split the band up and finish. I think the low point of the band was when Dave had his [personal] problems. At that time, for me, it seemed like there wasn't really any point in continuing. But fortunately Dave decided to make a change in his life, and since then, everything has been quite easy.

How did the new balance affect the making of *Ultra*?

This time around it was much more a team effort. I had an idea to work with Tim Simenon 'cause we'd known him for years, and he'd done a couple of remixes for us in the past. But we were totally unaware of the way he worked: He always works with the same team, which includes a programmer, a musician, and an engineer. In a way, Tim and his team helped to fill Alan's shoes. Alan was always the so-called musician in the band; the one who was classically trained. But it went far better [with Tim] than we ever could have imagined. We went into the studio to try out a couple of tracks just to see how things were, how we were getting on, how it would work with Tim as producer, and to test his team out. We didn't set ourselves any large goals. It was a question of trying out a few tracks, and maybe getting a single out of it, and

> **"I always start on guitar or piano, and get the basis of a song together before I move on to computers, keyboards, samplers, or whatever. I feel it's important to know that the song is strong before you get carried away with technology, because sometimes you fool yourself. You might think you've got a great song going, but in actual fact, what you're really liking is a synth sound or a bass line." —Martin Gore**

if things were going really well, then we could carry on and maybe make an album. So after the first recording session, about six weeks, it became very apparent that things were going well, and we decided to carry on with the whole project and make it into an album.

How did you write this batch of songs?

I think I still write in pretty much the same way as before. I always start on guitar or piano, and get the basis of a song together before I move on to computers, keyboards, samplers, or whatever. I feel it's important to know that the song is strong before you get carried away with technology, because sometimes you fool yourself. You might think you've got a great song going, but in actual fact, what you're really liking is a synth sound or a bass line. We've always been about songs — marrying songs with technology — and I think that sometimes that point gets lost. We often get cited as an influence by a lot of bands and producers, but it's more because we were an early electronic band, and more because of the *way* we created music as opposed to the actual songs.

Is melody usually the first element you focus on when writing?

Yeah, I think it is about melody, but it's also about emotion. If at the moment I sit down and write something and it moves me, I realize that there's a fairly good chance I might be able to move somebody else.

So after the initial piano/guitar writing phase, you sequence your song ideas.

Yeah. At home I've got a basic setup for demos. I've got [Hybrid Arts] ADAM machines for the recording, and I program on [Steinberg] Cubase. I use an Akai CD3000, a [Roland] JD-800, and a [Clavia] Nord Lead. The Nord is a very interesting synthesizer — the fact that you can record all your movements real time into the computer, wave sweeps and everything. I like it. I've also got three ARP 2600s and two Minimoogs. But I tend to keep things very basic at that stage.

How did your home versions translate to the studio sessions?

I made tapes and sent them out to Tim and the rest of the band, and then we went into the studio. It was a very different process for us this time. Sometimes there were three or four different things going on at once in the studio. There was a programmer, a musician, Tim, me, Dave, and sometime we might all be working on different things. Dave might be practicing his vocals, I might be doing something with Tim, the programmer might be working on a rhythm track, and the musician might be off working on a totally different track.

Did any of your demo tracks end up on the record, or were they all re-recorded?

It really differed from song to song. Sometimes the essence of what actually came out, what was released, was actually on the demo. But sometimes we totally pulled a song apart. If we felt that the basic song was good, but the direction of the demo wasn't quite right, we'd pull it apart and maybe reconstruct it three or four times before we were happy with it.

Taking a song like "Barrel of a Gun," for example, how similar was the final mix compared to the demo?

"Barrel of a Gun" was one that remained very similar to the original demo. All the parts were basically there, so it was just a question of bettering the sounds and making it a bit harder. But that was probably one of the most similar demos to the finished version.

The opening drum sequence is a real attention-getter. Is that a loop?

I think we originally started off with loops, and then tried to recreate them. It's very hard sometimes because a loop has an immediate atmosphere, but you don't always want to use a loop. So in this case it was a matter of recreating it by cutting up various loops to get snares and bass drum sounds.

***Ultra* is a down-tempo record. Any particular reason you kept everything under 100 beats per minute?**

It's the area that interests me the most at the moment. I find it emotional and moving at that tempo: 80 to 100 beats per minute. When I try writing anything faster than that, it just loses emotion for me. Maybe it's just a phase I'm going through [*laughs*].

Will the band be touring?

No, this is the first time ever that we've actually decided not to tour after finishing an album. We've toured on the back of every single album, and the last one was so long . . . we got to the end of it and were totally exhausted, mentally and physically. We had total communication breakdown problems within the band. We all hated each other. You know, that was the main reason Alan left. And so we don't want to repeat that again. We've just been in and out of the studio for 15 months, and the thought of going out on tour for a year is just too much to handle. We're considering, possibly, playing some live TV, but we're really trying to keep this year very stress-free. It's all questionable at the moment.

What's your take on the current resurgence of electronic music in the States?

We've been through quite a few electronic trends during our career, and one of the things we laugh about is the fact that it has absolutely no relevance to our record sales. Whether electronic music is in or not has no relevance to us. And I think it's because we created our own niche at a very early stage.

***[by Greg Rule*, Keyboard, July 1997]**

In 1998, Alan Wilder launched his solo attack under the name Recoil. Much speculation swirled around Wilder's departure from Depeche Mode, and what

Alan Wilder left
Depeche Mode
in 1995 to pursue
a solo career.
As Recoil, he
released the CD
Unsound Methods
in 1998.

the future held for him as a solo artist. As a member of the Mode, Wilder helped put synth pop on the map. His musicianship and sound-design skills were integral to the band's success. So why did he leave after the enormously successful *Songs of Faith and Devotion* record and tour? "I have no regrets," he says, frankly, "or any hard feelings about the group. I just didn't want to be in a pop group all my life. I certainly don't ever want to be in a group again. I think working in a particular format is something I'd done enough of. And there were other things I needed to sort out. Consequently I've come out on the other side much more fulfilled and enthusiastic and happy with my own life, and I'm very enthusiastic about making music."

Wilder's primary outlet for making music today is his side-project-turned-main-project Recoil and the CD *Unsound Methods* (Mute/Reprise) — a dark, moody, and very electronic collection. While reviews of the record were mixed, one sentiment seemed to be consistent: *Unsound Methods* is an album that must be listened to more than a few times to be appreciated. Alan is aware of this, but it doesn't seem to bother him. "I hear something that a lot of people don't seem to hear. I hear something that is quite instantly accessible. But I would say that because I made the music, and so for me it is instant. For everyone else, it takes time. Eventually, after hearing it eight or nine times, they start saying, 'I'm really getting into that album now.' I think it's very dynamic, diverse, and sinister, but not morbid and gloomy."

As with all Recoil records, the writing and recording process "have been simultaneous," he tells us. "I have nothing but a blank sheet of paper when I start. I work instinctively to react to the ideas, and if it gives me a particular kind of feeling, I'm moved from that point onwards. When I get a general theme or idea behind a track or story, the details come quite quickly. From there I get all of the tracks completed to a 70-percent stage, which could take anywhere from six to nine months. At that point, I think about who suits the song, or if it needs vocals at all. In this case the music was suggesting a lot of dialog. Then I go find people that I feel will be appropriate to fit the project."

Alan assembled vocalists Douglas McCarthy, Maggie Estep, Siobahn Lynch, and Hildia Campbell for the *Unsound* sessions. "They didn't drastically change the direction. They really helped enhance and focus it. Once the vocals were recorded, though, I did make a few adjustments to make sure it all worked together as a uniform piece. Sometimes that meant restructuring the music. Quite often I'd move choruses and verses around. I didn't change the words, but I restructured where they occurred."

Alan's attitude toward gear might surprise you. "I'm not the techno buff that a lot of people seem to think I am. I do have a healthy interest in production, and during my time with Depeche I was the one who was more involved with the shaping of sound, but it doesn't mean I'm that into technology. It means I'm enthusiastic about music and very interested in diversity of sound, but I'm not very technical. So I try to stick with equipment I'm comfortable with, that won't delay me with learning curves." Wilder's rig centers around Steinberg's Cubase running on a Mac. His samplers of choice are an Akai S3000 and S1100, and an E-mu EIII. "The hard disk side of Cubase is what I use mainly for vocals. Some of the synths I use are older Korgs that I inherited from Depeche when we split up the gear. I've got some analog gear, including a Minimoog and a MIDI Moog, an Oberheim OB rack, an ARP Odyssey, and an EMS synth. Then I've got various effects boxes. When I mix, I move all of the equipment to another studio which is more proper for a final mix. Although on the next project I'm determined to do the entire thing at home, which will require me to probably build a room and invest in a bit more equipment."

[by Robert Semrow, Keyboard, April 1998]

moog minimoog

*i*t was 1970 when the Minimoog first hit the streets, and 11 years later when Moog Music ceremoniously slapped brass plaques on the last 25 Minis off the assembly line and sent them out to fetch inflated prices. Yet the instrument's distinctive sound is very much with us today. In particular its fat, three-oscillator bass sound has transcended novelty and fashion and become a timbral staple, joining a small number of instruments — the Hammond B-3 organ and the Rhodes electric piano are two that come to mind — in the keyboard hall of fame.

A whole body of lore has built up around the Minimoog, ranging from which serial numbers sound the best to whether it is possible to accurately simulate its classic sound with a digital instrument. I'd like to separate the myths from the realities, and to comment on some of the instrument's enduring assets — as well as a few of its shortcomings. I was with Moog Music

vital stats

Description: Analog monophonic synthesizer.
Manufacturer: Moog Music, Buffalo, NY (out of business).
Production Dates: 1970-1981 (Serial numbers 1017-13259).
Approximate Number Made: 12,000.
Original Price: $1,495.

The most famous
monophonic synth
ever made: The
Moog Minimoog.
It's an essential
instrument in
Martin Gore's
studio rig.

when we put the first Minis into production, and I remained with the company until the end of 1977, so what I'm about to tell you is mostly first-hand testimony.

Back in 1969 and '70, Moog Music was not yet in the musical instrument business per se. Our modular synthesizers were sold as pieces of professional audio equipment. They were made to order, and we considered them to be too complex and high-tech to survive on the floor of a musical instrument store. Our original concept for the Minimoog was to take some of the basic features of our modular instruments and integrate them into a standard package that could be programmed without patchcords. We imagined that Minimoog customers would be session musicians who would welcome a synthesizer that could be carried to the gig. We figured that we might sell as many as a hundred Minis before it would be time to update the design.

The only Minimoog that was ever put into production is called the Model D. There were Models A, B, and C, but they were engineering prototypes. The first general public showing of the Model D was at the AES convention in the fall of 1970 — the same convention at which ARP unveiled their Model 2600.

Due to a change in Moog Music's management in 1971, we had the opportunity to exhibit the Model D at the 1971 NAMM show in Chicago. Most of the dealers didn't know what to make of a musical instrument with words like "Oscillator Bank" and "Filter" printed on the front panel. But to be honest, it wasn't all the dealers' fault. Although we could explain how the Minimoog worked, we couldn't demo it with convincing musicianship. Little by little, however, word got around to musicians that the Minimoog was a worthy axe. Keith Emerson nailed its analog sound into the vocabulary of rock and roll, first on his modular behemoth and then on his Mini. Then came Jan Hammer, who developed incredible chops with the left-hand wheels. In less than two years, Minimoogs were being sold and played around the world, and Moog Music had a staff of salespeople who called on its expanding dealer network.

The Model D became Moog Music's first standard production instrument. By the latter part of 1973, production had increased from a few instruments a week to a peak of 300 Minis a month. This required a change in manufacturing techniques — especially in the areas of testing and quality control. Throughout those early years, Moog manufacturing's professionalism increased steadily. I'm not mentioning this to pat myself on the back. In fact, I personally had almost nothing to do with manufacturing back then. The reason I'm mentioning the steady improvement is to contrast it with the electronic folk tale that says that the earliest Minimoogs were better because they had more "human element." I've heard this story more times than I care to admit. Don't believe it! Of course, Minimoogs, like most analog instruments, do vary somewhat from instrument to instrument, so you may find an old Minimoog with really great sound and a minimum of reliability problems (the first one, serial no. 1017, was released in 1970), but overall, the later instruments are much more reliable, and they sound better too!

We never did get to improve on the functional design of the Minimoog. There were, however, many manufacturing design changes, the most important of which was a new oscillator board that provided greatly improved stability. All instruments with serial numbers greater than 10175 have this new board.

In addition, many older instruments had new oscillator boards retrofitted in the field.

After 1974, small analog synthesizers appeared on the market in great profusion, and Minimoog sales began to decline. By 1980, microprocessor-controlled polyphonic analog synths were all the rage. Moog Music decided to stop manufacturing the Mini, partly because the new microprocessor-controlled Moog Source was intended to fill the Mini's slot in the marketplace. The last 25 Minimoogs off the production line were deluxe instruments, with solid walnut cases (just like the very first Minis), illuminated wheels, and numbered brass plaques. The last one made (serial no. 13259) was given to me at a press luncheon at the 1981 NAMM convention in Chicago.

By 1983, digital instruments with MIDI interfaces were stealing the show, and for a while, analog sounds were out of favor. Now they're back in, especially the Minimoog bass sounds. During the mid-'80s, it was possible to pick up a Mini on the used market for under $300 (the original price was $1,495). Nowadays, we've seen Minis selling for well over $1,000. And if you live in Europe, we've heard the going rate is much higher.

[by Bob Moog, Keyboard, September 1989]

vince clarke of erasure

Electro-Luddite

*i*t's as catchy as a cold, and stocked with more hooks than a block and tackle shop. But it ain't simple: The music of Vince Clarke, all points and pops behind the seraphic vocals of Andy Bell in Erasure, is riddled with contradiction. Pinprick sequences spin; textures are all quick jabs, pad-free. Yet somehow it flows like mercury, cool and smooth. Chords are solid, the bass always locked to the root, but textures shimmer; listening to Erasure is like watching Gibraltar, showered in tinsel, sparkle in sunlight.

The enigma of Erasure is especially evident on the duo's smash album *I Say, I Say, I Say* — an ultra-pure product with nothing but voice and analog synths. No samples, no FM. On the other hand, there's no acoustic instrumentation, and practically no real-time playing. You won't find a more electronic album or a cleaner production in the bins, but the sound harks back to Human League, OMD, and early Depeche Mode, Clarke's original band. Is it modern rock? Or nostalgia for the stone age of synth rock?

And what of Clarke himself? Face-to-face, he's an amiable guy. Short red hair, two gold earrings, orange tortoise-shell specs. Warm, slightly cockeyed smile.

Vince Clarke of Erasure (R) first arrived on the synth pop scene as a member of Depeche Mode during the *Speak and Spell* era.
◄···························

Quick and ironic wit. As with his music, something solid lies beneath a glittery veneer. He has no problem demonstrating his primitive chops with graceless, stiff-fingered pokes. He also knows what he likes, and holds nothing back in expressing his beliefs.

Here, again, we have contradictions: Clarke is an analog purist who has serious problems with the vintage synth revival. He's a painstaking perfectionist, capable of lingering over note after note in his step-input sequences. Yet he describes his approach as improvisational, based in large degree on mystery and what might be described as a kind of voluntary ignorance. More even than the sound, the process of analog synthesis appeals to him — the knob twiddles, the exploration, the alchemy.

From its genesis in the '70s, synth rock has evolved toward dark horizons. The path from Kraftwerk to techno has few detours or interruptions; the quest for precision, the purge of human clutter and the triumph of the computer groove, has created a consensus that alienation is the most, perhaps the only, appropriate emotion to cultivate in sequence-based, dance-oriented music. Clarke is one of the very few artists to challenge that notion. In fact, he's been defying it for nearly 14 years, since the release of *Speak and Spell*. That album established Depeche Mode as masters of cheery, upbeat electro-pop before the band parted ways with Clarke to join the rest of the synth-rock herd in its gloom-bound trudge.

After leaving Depeche Mode, Clarke recorded several highly regarded albums with Alison "Alf" Moyet as Yazoo, released a British hit single, "Never Never," in a project called The Assembly, and eventually found himself auditioning singers for what turned out to be Erasure. Andy Bell got the call; his voice, a kind of Brit echo of Aaron Neville, perfectly complemented Clarke's staccato sensibility. Their first album, *Wonderland*, established the formula in 1986: crisp, percolating arpeggios swirling around choir boy vocals, undergirded by the mean stomp of synthesized drums.

Other albums and several dance club hits followed, but by the late '80s Clarke and Bell were making their biggest waves onstage. Even Depeche Mode couldn't match their impact: They sold out Madison Square Garden in two hours, drew 50,000 fans to the Milton Keynes Bowl, played 15 consecutive nights at both the Manchester Apollo and the Hammersmith Odeon. Fifty thousand spectators gathered one night in Buenos Aires to watch an Erasure video. This was Springsteen/Jackson territory — pretty heady stuff for a band that didn't even have a guitar player.

At the time of this writing, Clarke and Bell were about to begin work on another album, with plans to make it their second release of the year. Ex-Human Leaguer Martyn Ware, who produced *I Say, I Say, I Say,* had the inside track for this project as well. But no matter who controls the console, Clarke will once more fan the creative flame and keep the analog banner clean.

What distinguishes *I Say, I Say, I Say* from previous Erasure albums?

It has a particular kind of purity because we did all the vocals first. The music came last. We recorded with a very basic track, just the chord arrangement, on tape, to which Andy did all his harmonies and lead vocals. Then I put the music around the singing. Normally, it's the other way around.

Was the songwriting process different as well?

No. We always write together acoustically.

Why did you reverse the recording routine?

Really, just to see what would happen. I suppose we had the idea that it might be a more vocal-oriented album. We had all these grand ideas about using Andy's voice to do rhythms and stuff, because we don't use samplers. But that didn't work out.

He really holds on to the melody on this album, as if he wasn't being distracted by or interacting with your parts.

That's right. I think he has a hard time sometimes because he listens to the track when we do that first, but he's not really listening to the music. He'll have a harmony idea or a counter-melody idea that will be so strong in his head that it won't matter if it's some synth music or if there's a funny noise in the middle of it; he'll just do it over the top of it. That causes problems sometimes, and we have to take out a piece of music. This way around, I could just put the music around his singing. We went to Dublin for a few weeks; he did all the vocals there. Then we came back to London to do the music.

What kinds of demos did you do?

We just had a piano, with Andy singing.

With some sort of rhythm?

No, no rhythm. We never put a style into the demo. What we usually do, kind of deliberately, is record them as crappily as possible. And it's always on a microcassette. We've only got one. We've demoed five albums on this thing, over and over. That's important for us, because when we're writing, we try to make the song as good as possible. That's it.

The guitar mentality is quite different from the keyboard mentality: You hit the notes differently, you play different kinds of chords. Is there much of your previous life as a guitar player left in the way you create music on synths?

I switch between the two modes. When I'm writing songs, all I'm thinking about is chord structures: What sounds nice with the melody in the background of the song? Sometimes, when I'm sequencing in the studio, I'll try and imagine what a guitar might play — not necessarily the sounds or the bad timing, but the harmonic and rhythmic parts. I'm a terrible guitarist, by the way.

There are some guitar-like figures on this album.

I can do that. If I arpeggiate a song in, like, eighth-notes, then I'll arpeggiate it how I'd pick a guitar.

Do you play those parts on guitar?

No. Everything I do is step-time.

Not too many people work that way anymore.

Well, I use very old-fashioned sequencers. When it comes to the arrangement and getting the track out, I'll use this BBC Micro computer. The software for it is UMI, which doesn't exist anymore. The guy wrote the program in his bedroom; it's very much a home thing. Once I've got the arrangement going and all the sounds happening, I transfer the information in real time, one monophonic line at a time, into a Roland MC-4. I'll do that through a Roland MPU-101, and then we'll record from the MC-4.

You've used that method for quite some time.

Right. It used to be a pain in the ass, because then you'd have to program the MC-4s. It's a nightmare: The display is only this big, and it only shows one thing — the note, the gate, the step, or something. It takes forever. But now I'll get the arrangement up in a MIDI sequencer, the UMI, and I'll use the MC-4 just to record with.

You've stayed with the BBC platform as well.

They're not made anymore either. The BBC was actually developed for people in schools to learn very simple software writing.

Why haven't you made the leap to a more widely used computer?

Well, I started out using MC-4s. Then MIDI sequencers came out with the Yamaha QX1, but they were so expensive. UMI was the first MIDI sequencer that had a screen: You could see more than one piece of information at a time.

Was it a black-and-white screen?

It was then, but then it developed. The guy updates the software all the time. Then Atari came out, and it wiped him off the map. He still does it for me, though. I can't do Ataris. I can't take them seriously. I can't!

What do you like about the UMI program?

It's like a drum machine sequencer. You work with your hands. I can't get my mind around tape recorder sequencers like Cubase. I don't get it.

Is the support there if your system crashes?

Yeah, because the guy still does things for me. He doesn't do it to make a living anymore, but I can get him to write software for me. It's essentially like a cheap little computer. I used to use UMI for everything, but I use the MC-4 now to actually record with. And I use a custom-built, six-channel ARP sequencer. I've got a few ARPs.

How do you feel about the vintage keyboard phenomenon?

Well, everybody's cashing in on analog now. It's funny. People might say that an analog synthesizer is better than a modern synthesizer because it's got a classic sound. But I don't think that's the point. The point in using something like a Serge Modular system is that you've got so many knobs to twiddle around with and change. There are no rules, no preset modulations. You can do anything you like with it, and you never know what's going to come out at the end. So people miss out on the joys of doing that if they use one of those Vintage Keys things.

The process is the point, even more than the sound.

It is for me.

Yet you've got a sampling CD out on the market.

Well, I'm not really up for sampling, but this kid phoned me up with the idea of putting out a collection of my analog sounds. He was so enthusiastic! He could have been a car salesman, he was that convincing. He had his own tiny company called AMG; he makes these things in his bedroom. So he came to my studio in Amsterdam, and we spent two days with someone else who operated a DAT machine. I just messed about, running sequences and changing the sounds, and they recorded the bits they liked. The only problem was that we had to get 500 sounds. After a while, they all started sounding the same to me [*laughs*]. But I did it because this bloke was so funny. He's such a sweet little lad. I was thinking of doing another one of funny sounds. There's nothing more satisfying than making a synthesizer sound like a fart.

What's the best synth for funny sounds?

[*Instant response.*] ARP 2600.

But now these sounds are going to wind up in people's samplers, untweaked. You're just contributing to the problem you've diagnosed in modern synthesis.

[*Bemused shrug.*] Yeah, well, you know.

Most synth bands that base their music largely on sequences and dance beats seem to create an industrial or angst-ridden feel. But you use these same devices to create a warmer, more romantic feeling, without resorting to new agey pads or clichés. How do you humanize these devices?

I think it comes down to not thinking about it. That's what makes it work. I approach music very simply because, first of all, I can't play very well. So I don't overcomplicate things. And using things like ARP sequencers is a random process. Also, instead of using block chords, I do lots of interweaving lines from synthesizers. That's more interesting, and things turn out more melodic that way.

That arpeggiation combines the static effect of the chords with a kind of shimmering dynamic sense. The key, in this approach, is to work with the details of each sequence.

Absolutely. You look at every single note and every single sound. That's really important. You're not dealing with a line that just fills the song. You're not looking at a stereo pad that is the bulk of the song. I don't even like the word "pad." In the studio we have a swear system: There are certain words you can't say, otherwise you pay a 50 pence fine. "Pad" is one of them.

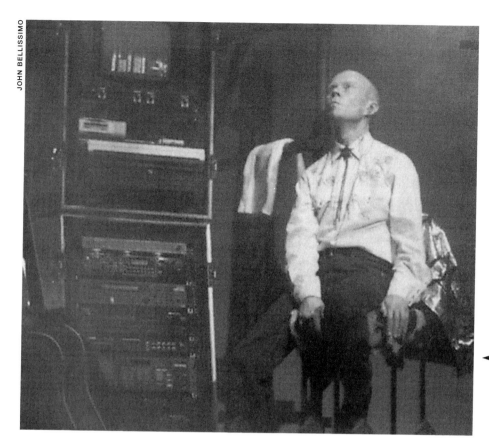

Happy trails. Clarke onstage during Erasure's 1997 *Cowboy* tour.

What else?

You can't say "MIDI." You can't say "digital." You can't say "SSL." You can say them outside the studio, not inside.

How about "touch-sensitive"?

I don't use it, so that wouldn't come up.

"Polyphonic"?

That's okay.

"Sampling"?

That's very bad. We also have the mystery word of the day: That would be worth a pound. There's always three of us in the studio. If one of us is late, he misses out on the mystery word, which would be written on a piece of paper but turned the wrong way around. We'd just add up how many times he'd say it, then present a bill to him at the end of the day.

Apparently traditional keyboard parts never appealed to you.

I could never do that, even if I wanted to. My synthesizer background is doing this [*Clarke jabs alternating notes an octave apart, using two stiff forefingers*] with Depeche Mode, since it was all monophonic anyway. It's never gotten much better than that.

What is your keyboard of choice for playing those sorts of parts?

I don't actually play keyboards at all anymore. Everything is sequenced. My favorite synthesizers change all the time. Every synthesizer in my studio is analog. There's a few FM things downstairs in the junk room. I never understood FM programming anyway. It's the same with samplers: Someone comes along with their sample disc, and it's like, "Gimme that," and you try to find a sound that fits: bass drums, snare drums, or whatever. It's so boring! I've tried to program new synths, but you spend half an hour trying to doctor a sound and make it interesting. Then, when you do the comparison, the sound that the guy in Japan came up with is a hundred times better. So there's no pleasure in it. Then, of course, if I'm using their sounds, so are a hundred other people. So I've gotten rid of everything, and I've been buying up all of America's analog synthesizers. I only buy them here.

They're too expensive in the U.K.?

You just can't get them there. I've become a mad collector of stuff. Things keep cropping up all the time. The last thing I got was a Buchla system, with about 16 modules in the cabinet. It's very old and knackered. But I'm getting it fixed. They look great in the studio as well.

Some of the vocal parts on this album sound like samples.

[*Firmly.*] There are no samples. We used a choir on two tracks. When we were in Dublin, we went to a cathedral and recorded their choir in stereo. They were the real thing.

On "So the Story Goes," the choir seems to go out of tune toward the end.

That was our wanky producer's idea. He said, "Wouldn't it be great if they went out of key on this?" And we said, "Well, I'm not interested in vocals anyway, so whatever you want" [*laughs*].

What kind of impact did your producer, Martyn Ware, have?

He's a very enthusiastic producer. He hadn't made a synthesizer record for 15 years or something; I suppose the last one was with Heaven 17, but even they

"I like drum sounds that sound like synthesizers. I like music that sounds like clockwork. I prefer my music coming from the moon."

weren't really doing synthesizer music at the end. Before that, he was in The Human League, which was real synthesizer music — *Travelogue* and *Reproduction* [Virgin, both out of print]. So his enthusiasm spilled over into the album. He was open; he wasn't trying to make us into anything we weren't. Just let us get on with it. I mean, he was still in control, because if we were left to our own devices, the record would never finish.

What did you use for drum sounds on the album?

It's all modular systems. I don't have to rely on anybody's samples; I get my own drum sounds.

There are practically no acoustically resonant drum sounds in your work.

I like drum sounds that sound like synthesizers. I like music that sounds like clockwork. I prefer my music coming from the moon.

A good example of that clockwork approach is in "Because You're So Sweet." Why did you add a few extra bars of what sounds like a wound-up mechanical clock in the midst of this romantic ballad?

You know how a real band plays when they put a little pause after a drum fill? I'm not really a muso [musician], so I don't really know what the expression is, but it's kind of a tension thing. We just decided that it would be nice to have something like that at this point of the song, but doing it electronically is a pain in the ass. If you do one or two bars with the synchronizer, you've got to change the tempo. This was literally the sequence slowing down, going from tempo 108 to 80.

There's an eight-bar percussion break in "Blues Away" that features at least some suggestions of acoustical resonance, in a kind of industrial style.

Again, it was me just messing about. I usually work in the studio on my own to get things going before the producer comes in. At that point in the song, I just triggered the ARP sequencers to kick off. I had two ARP sequencers running, and I was using white noise and pink noise to modulate filters.

Andy's very human vocals apparently balance out that approach. Do you ever want to do a solo project that goes farther toward the style you're describing?

Not really. I mean, we work solo together. The way that we balance off of each other is a real pleasure. And it's nice when you've got someone else there saying, "Yeah, that's a really interesting sound." It would be very difficult for me to do it on my own.

How do your arrangements evolve from the acoustic demos? Let's use "Miracle" as an example.

Well, all the tracks on this album are better arranged than anything we've ever done. Once the songs were written and demoed on the piano, we did the rough arrangement in Amsterdam; that was with the producer. Usually, when we write a song, we've got three or four melodic parts, each one four or eight bars long. We just join the pieces together: "That could be the chorus. That could be the bridge. Is that repeatable or not? That bit can only be used once." Then, when we have the vocals recorded, it comes time to do the music for real. Now, there's a thin whiny sound that goes all the way through "Miracle." I think it's a Roland MS-20 that arpeggiates the basic chords.

The interlocking sequences are an Erasure trademark.

That's not being done much in arrangements anymore, and I think that's because the limitation is that it has to be a dance track: The drums have to be in from the very beginning, all the time. That's a real shame. We never set out to make this album a dance record. They're just songs, so we could do whatever we pleased with the arrangements.

Is the backbeat emphasized too much in modern synthesizer rock?

It's just the type of music that's being done. People who make dance music aren't writing songs. It's not about classic songs that will be covered in 50 years; they're just dance tracks. So I suppose it has to be that way for them.

Were you interested in techno when it came out?

I really don't know anything about it. I'm completely ignorant.

It seems to have established itself so quickly that a set of clichés is already restricting much of its development.

Yeah. You get a production team, and they'll always use the same riff from the same record in every song that they remix. I've cut away from that. We have remixes done of our tracks, and I don't listen to them. It's not something that interests me. I like to go to clubs, but not that much.

What about ambient techno?

I quite like some ambient music when I hear it, although I don't know what I'm listening to. I did just rebuy [Brian Eno's] *Music for Airports*.

Did the idea of found sounds in the form of samples ever appeal to you as an arrangement device?

No. Again, by that time I was bored with those multi-purpose buttons that you have on samplers. I was fed up with trying to find the right thing on the right menu and all that crap. Used to piss me off.

You have used drum samples before — for example, on your cover of "River Deep, Mountain High," from *The Innocents.*

But things have evolved over the past two or three albums. We've moved away from that. This album is pure synth.

You've abandoned other elements that appeared on earlier albums. There were piano sounds, for example, on *The Innocents.*

It's actually an acoustic guitar on a couple of tracks.

"Take Me Back" does have an organ-like sound in the three-chord structural figure. Or does it sound that way to you?

I don't know! I never intentionally program keyboards to sound like anything. I'm just tweaking 'em until I get the right dryness or the right dullness or whatever — until it fits in. I would shy away from saying, "What we need here is a brass-type sound."

Your bass part is almost always on the root of the chord. Only on the chorus in "Miracle" does it climb up to the 3rd of one chord.

I don't know what else to do [*laughs*]!

Why did you go up to that 3rd on "Miracle"?

That was probably the producer's idea; it wouldn't be mine. I know it's terrible, but for me it's "always stick to the root." One reason is that, on a lot of tracks, we've not got a lot of chords. There's nothing establishing the chord, so you've got to start somewhere, and I let the bass in to give you an indication.

Real bass players would be moving lines all over the place.

Well, I don't know what bass players do. I'm not a bass player myself, so I have no idea.

There were some almost Beatlesque touches on "Man in the Moon," including backwards string sounds.

They probably came from the Oberheim Xpander. The rhythm track on that one was mostly done with the [Roland] System 100M. I've got this six-channel ARP sequencer, which I use like a drum machine. It's got 16 steps on it. I connect that to my System 100Ms. Then I get it to clock 'round and 'round, put the switches up for the different beats or whatever I'm doing, work on one channel, then the next, then the next, hitting different sounds up. It becomes a rhythm track to the music. It's a really easy way of working.

What about the bagpipish feel in the intro to "All Through the Years"?

That was the Xpander. The whiny thing at the top came because I had just seen a program about Professor Theremin. I was trying to emulate that.

There's one spot on the album, on "Because You're So Sweet," where the synth plays a lead line — the melody, actually.

It just seemed like the right thing to do. The arrangement is very simple: verse, chorus, verse, chorus, middle eight, and chorus out. So it just felt right. I used an Oberheim SEM [voice module]; it can be quite a mellow-sounding synth.

You do seem to have limited the range of sounds you work with on _I Say, I Say_. Aside from samples, there's no deep bass or filtery string patches.

That wasn't planned either. When we work in the studio, it's like being in a toy shop. I've got all this analog stuff, and it all interconnects. I'll go mad in there. I'll know what I'm doing, but I'm not planning it particularly.

Do you remember your sound sources after the record is done?

No. I know that the bass drums usually come from the ARP 2600.

So how do you prepare to reproduce these songs onstage?

It's a nightmare. It took me longer to program for the last tour than it took me to do the album because none of these synthesizers has a memory. Once you've written the next song, that's it. You're finished. I couldn't take my modular Moogs on tour, so I scattered things out and used Prophet-5s, Junos, Jupiters,

"MIDI is so out of time. It's crap. It gives you a constantly sloshy sound. I can't stand it."

stuff like that. I took on equivalent sounds. On a track I may have 16 musical things happening. I use an MC-4 live, so I brought all of that down to four synthesizers and got rid of the things I felt I wouldn't necessarily need.

Which four synths did you take on the road?

I had an Oberheim Xpander, a Jupiter JP-8, a Minimoog for bass, and a Sequential Prophet-5.

No MIDI?

No MIDI.

Why not?

It's so out of time. It's crap. It gives you a constantly sloshy sound. I can't stand it. On the album before this one, we started using scopes to scope the timings of every sound. A click track would go on one channel. Then you'd feed the sound through the other channel, so you could change the timing of the bass drum to fall exactly on the point of the click. Every sound was scoped. You can't do that with MIDI, because it's a bit irregular.

I take it you've never added any MIDI retrofits to older gear.

I've had MIDI retrofits taken out. On things like the OB rack and the rack Moog.

Why spend the money to take it out? Why not just ignore it?

It's just my puritannical view of MIDI.

Why not sample the sounds you need for concerts?

It would take too long. Besides, when I'm preparing for a tour, I'm not trying to reproduce exactly. So, in a way, preparing for a tour is quite artistic as well. I'm doing new interpretations of the songs, getting sounds. I might base it on what I've recorded, but I'm messing about.

If you don't play keyboards anymore, what will you do onstage for the next tour?

For the last tour, I drove around in a tank with all my keyboards in the roof. I had a telly fit inside it, and I watched that. Everything was sequenced; I had my headphones geared to my television so I wouldn't miss the cues: "Next song!"

Isn't there a risk that audiences will be disappointed at not seeing a performance onstage?

Most people who go to concerts, whatever the music might be, aren't particularly musos. They don't have a clue what anybody's doing up onstage. They like the band or the music, and that's it. If you say, "That's a great bass sound on that record," a lot of punters wouldn't know what the bass is. They're interested in singing the song in the bathroom or the shower; that's what's important to them.

[by Robert L. Doerschuk, Keyboard, September 1994]

For fans of live music, there's nothing quite like seeing your favorite artist who typically plays amphitheaters in a smaller and more intimate venue. Erasure gave their fans just such a thrill in 1997, performing a string of small-venue warm-up shows before launching their summer/fall full-scale tour. In a previous conversation with Vince Clarke, he indicated Erasure might not ever tour again. So when I caught up with him prior to the Los Angeles warm-up show, I asked him what changed the band's mind.

"We weren't going to tour again. It's not a healthy lifestyle. We got so sick of it. What happened was, we were in the States a few years ago and we were going around doing radio promotions with acoustic guitar. We invited some people from the fan club to a club in New York for an evening with Erasure. We did some acoustic songs, and I just felt that the reaction was really good. Everyone was asking about us going back on tour."

The choice to start out in smaller venues was equally surprising. "It was because we haven't toured in a couple of years," said Clarke. "We weren't sure that we could pack out anywhere. So this was really like a testing of water." And a successful test it was.

On tour with Vince that time around were an Oberheim Matrix-6R, a Roland SH-101, MKS-50, MKS-70, MKS-80, and JV-1080, a Novation Drumstation, an E-mu Proteus, and a Waldorf Pulse — all being run by a BBC Micro. "I have a CV-to-MIDI converter on it because it was too unwieldy to use analog sequences for this particular tour. But we're sticking with my old BBC, which is now over

15 years old." Vince also familiarized himself with the digital world he used to shun. "I don't really understand it. What I'm trying to do is replicate sounds that I get in the studio. It's quite hard to do that. But with something like the JV-1080, it's seems that there are a million sounds in it. So I spent weeks just plodding through each sound."

Despite the smaller venue, Erasure once again demonstrated their flair for stage props, which included a campfire, a hotel, a stagecoach, a saloon, picket fences, multiple costume changes by the band, and a huge tower of Vince's synth modules and computer gear. Vince seemed to enjoy climbing up the supports for the gear, occasionally making adjustments while running the music from his command post.

While he chose not to display his keyboard techniques this time around (the computer handled that), he still managed to hold the crowd's interest — in particular, he dressed up in a cactus outfit, played his guitar, and danced around. Yee-haw!

The set list consisted of many old hits along with a few songs from the new album *Cowboy* (Maverick). The new versions of the classics were fresh and energetic, and they kept the audience dancing and singing throughout the hour-and-a-half show. As for singer Andy Bell, he was and always is at his best in front of an adoring audience. As Vince commented, "I think what happens is that when he gets onstage, he becomes somebody else. He never fails to surprise me. Whether it's the things he says or does, it's always entertaining for me and the crowd. I think people appreciate that we don't take ourselves too seriously." Whether it was doing their rendition of "Singin' in the Rain," or gathering around the campfire to sing, Erasure genuinely appeared to be having fun.

Cowboy marks a return to the emotional, energetic pop songs that the band is so well known for. "We decided that for this album we would write all short songs and we did. We wrote more than we needed, which is unusual for us. I think we're regressing, actually [*laughter*]."

Progressively regressing, I think.

[by Robert Semrow, Keyboard, October 1997]

sequential prophet-5

the date: January 1978. The place: The Disneyland Hotel in Anaheim, California. The event: The winter NAMM (National Association of Music Merchant show. Moog and ARP were revelling in their heyday — synth-industry giants in the days when Roland and Yamaha were still trying to figure out how to make a synthesizer that would sell in the U.S.

Tom Oberheim's modular 4- and 8-voice synths, Moog's Polymoog, and ARP's two-voice 2600 were about the only synthesizers able to sound more than one note at a time (other than by putting out unison chords). The Oberheim was the only polyphonic synth with the capacity to remember patches, but it couldn't store all of its parameters in memory.

Two landmarks were unveiled at this particular NAMM show. Yamaha's John Gates previewed the CS-80, an 8-voice polyphonic synth with the first polyphonic

The wood-paneled
Prophet-5 was
(and still is) a
favorite of
many synth
superstars,
including
Vince Clarke.

aftertouch keyboard and hard-wired memory capability. Meanwhile, tucked away in a tiny booth on the lower level of the convention facility, a barely working prototype of the Prophet-5 was being shown by Dave Smith, former Moog clinician John Bowen, and businesswoman Barb Fairhurst — the staff of Sequential Circuits, a self-funded outfit that started in the confines of Smith's San Jose, California, garage selling a digital sequencer and a generic programmer.

Sequential was hardly the kind of mega company you'd expect to send industry leaders running for cover, but while Moog and ARP were battling over the relative merits of pitchbend wheels vs. ribbons vs. spongy little rectangles called PPCs (proportional pressure controllers), Sequential was cranking out the kind of instrument, with the kind of sound and features, that musicians needed.

By today's standards, those features may look a bit lacking — a whopping 40 user-programmable presets (later revs had 120 programs), five non-multitimbral voices, a non-touch-sensitive keyboard, etc. But the Prophet was the first synth in which every parameter could be stored in computer memory.

Its voice architecture, contrary to popular myth, had more in common with the ARP Odyssey voice than with the Minimoog, since it featured two audio oscillators per voice, with its third oscillator being a dedicated LFO. The VCO pulse width was continuously variable, and the two envelope generators were ADSRs.

If there was a single feature that defined the Prophet sound, it was the poly-mod section, which enabled you to use the filter envelope and osc 2 to modulate the frequency of the pulse-width of osc 1, and/or the filter cutoff frequency. These modulation routings, combined with osc 1's sync function, produced the trademark (and at one time hopelessly overused) oscillator sweeping sync sound, usually variations of what was originally factory preset 33.

There have been a number of different models of the Prophet, each a slight improvement (theoretically) from the last version or revision (rev for short). The original Prophets came be known as rev 1. Few of these have survived over the years, because they were handbuilt, but the serious bench testing for quality was implemented much later. The rev 1 model was sent out the door as quickly as possible so Smith and company could pay their bills. As a result, it was a buggy and fragile beast. You can generally tell a rev 1 from a rev 2 by the reddish Koa wood used for its case (most of the 2 and 3 revs used a walnut case). Other distinguishing features were the placement of the power on/off switches: They're on the front panel of rev 1, and the back panel of rev 2. The rev 3 featured cassette interface controls on the front panel.

In addition to these physical characteristics are sonic differences. The rev 1 and 2 have a fatter, ballsier sound than rev 3. SSM chips were used in 1 and 2, while Curtis chips were used in later models because they were consistent and reliable.

The rev 1 didn't have a cassette interface for storage, though chances are any rev you find today will have this feature. Auto-tuning was accomplished by pressing program select switches 1 and 8 simultaneously on rev 1. Editing a parameter required pushing two switches simultaneously, after which turning a knob would add to or subtract from the value as stored in memory. On the rev 2, this system was changed so that turning a knob would instantly jump the parameter to the absolute setting, overriding whatever was in memory.

The circuit board placement was changed with the rev 2 design, so they are easier to service than the rev 1. For example, in order to do a routine cleaning of the keyboard contacts in a rev 1, you have to remove the circuit board with the Z-80 on it. If you accidentally plug that in backwards, you end up with a fried processor. Ouch. Rev 3 included the ability to alter the tuning of each note in an octave and store this setting as part of a patch.

Rev 3.2 or 3.3 machines were the only units be MIDI'd. MIDI implementations range from basic (omni mode only) to extensive (poly mode, 16-channel assignments, program change commands, pitchbend wheel in three ranges, and data dumps). Six versions of MIDI software were done in all. Interestingly, none of them supported the mod wheel; there just wasn't enough room left in ROM.

Sequential marketed a digital polyphonic sequencer that connected directly to the rev 3 via a pre-MIDI proprietary serial digital bus that was 30 times faster than MIDI. Only a few hundred of these were made, according to Dave Smith. They sold new for about $1,300.

[by Mark Vail, Keyboard, February 1990]

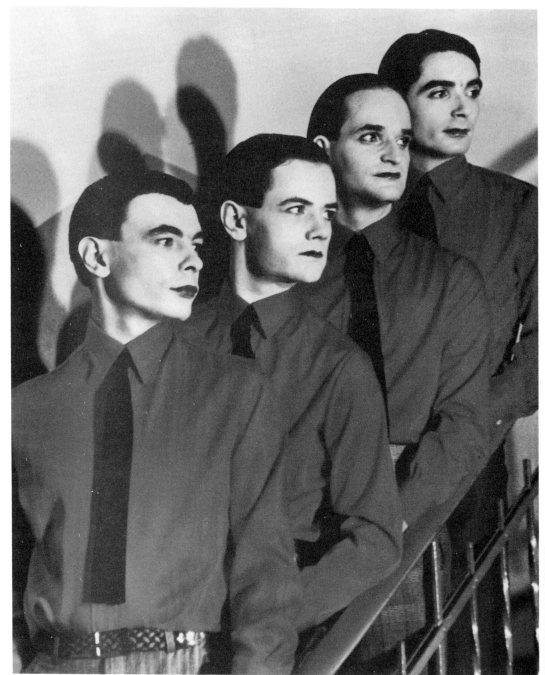

kraftwerk

Architects of the Trans-Global Express

Once upon a time, "the future" was something that hadn't happened yet. It lay up ahead of us somewhere in the distance, filled with an unknown potential whose features and even outlines were unguessable. But during the 20th century, an extremely odd thing happened. In the 1920s, science fiction writers began developing detailed scenarios of what the future would be like, and after World War II the technology for making those scenarios come true expanded at an unprecidented rate. By now our sense of history as a linear progression into the future has collapsed. We're living in the future today.

Most of us have ambivalent feelings about the future. On the one had, we're happy to take advantage of the products and processes it offers. We get instant cash from automatic bank machines, play with video games, use articles made of plastic and other synthetic materials dozens of times a day, talk to our relatives long distance via satallite relay, and hop on jets that take us to other continents in mere hours. But on the other hand, the future makes us uneasy — sometimes very uneasy. We're not happy about having computerized dossiers on our private lives hidden in secret government memory banks. We're disturbed by the way eight-lane freeways (to say nothing of strip-mines) deface the landscape. We yearn for simple answers to the bewildering complex social problems that

It was the synthetic sound heard 'round the world: Kraftwerk's cold, robotic records forever changed the face of electronic pop music.
◄·····················

erupt at every turn. We want to feel that we're important and unique as individuals, not just faceless, interchangeable units in a giant machine.

The message is that we can develop a friendly, relaxed, accepting attitude toward working and living with machines. Most of us still feel obscurely threatened by machines — "depersonalized" and "mechanical" are dirty words. According to Kraftwerk spokesman Ralf Hutter, "America is very shy when it comes to electronics. It's still a highly schizophrenic situation. People have all the latest state-of-the-art technology, and yet they put wood panels on the front to help them feel comfortable. Or they develop new plastics and try to imitate the appearance of wood. They use modern technology to try to recreate the Middle Ages. This is stupid." In contrast, Kraftwerk's custom-built musical equipment looks like what it is. "We go more for the minimalist or direct approach," Hutter explains. "Technology as an art — technology as it is. We have nothing to hide."

This attitude has obvious roots in the Bauhaus school of functionalist architecture that flourished in the 1920s, in which pipes, wiring, and girders were frequently exposed rather than hidden behind walls. But Kraftwerk's preoccupation with technology stems more directly from the predominantly industrial environment of Dusseldorf in the 1950s and '60s, where Hutter and co-founder Florian Schneider grew up. Although their music today seems to be firmly based in pop, they both studied traditional classical music at the Dusseldorf Conservatory — Hutter studying piano and Schneider flute — and then moved on to performing improvised avant-garde music. "At that time," Hutter recalls, "the only places we could find to play were at universites and art museums. Musical clubs wouldn't book us. The music world is very reactionary, isn't it? It's all about ticket sales.

"The first problem we faced," he goes on, "was to find the type of music we wanted to play. So we started out with pure sound. Florian had an amplified flute, and I had some contact microphones which I put on metal plates. Also, we used to put contact mikes on my clothing so that the sounds I made by moving were part of the music." Even at this early stage, they were breaking down the barriers between performer and instrument, between man and machine.

One of the reasons they stopped using conventional instruments (an early incarnation of Kraftwerk, prior to 1974, actually had a guitarist) was that these instruments imply conventional relationships between the performer and the instrument, and thus produce a conventional sort of music with which the listener then has a conventional relationship. In place of this, Hutter and Schnieder have experimented with using such unusual interfaces as beams of light that could be interrupted to trigger musical effects with the body. The ultimate, they feel, would be an instrument that "instantly produces whatever sound you think of" by a direct link with the mind. This would imply a complete symbiosis of organism and technology.

In 1970 Hutter and Schneider established their own recording studio, which they called Kling Klang, a German word that means just what you think it means. Hutter owned a Farfisa organ, and in 1971 they aquired their first synthesizers. A Minimoog, we asked? An ARP 2600? Hutter was vague. "Yeah, mostly those," he replied. "We had all the small models from all the different major brands. We had an English one [an EMS Synthi]. Sometimes they were very nice. But they don't make them anymore. Today they are already antiques. By now we have sold them or given them to other people." Most of their equipment today is custom-built.

During the next few years they released several albums that were distributed only in Europe. But popular acceptance was slow. "Germany is a cultural vacuum," Hutter explains. "All the music on the radio was Anglo-American when we started. We had a German name and we sang in German, so they wouldn't play us on the radio. People were very upset, because nobody was supposed to do this kind of thing. We didn't have a living music of our own in Germany. It has only been in the last ten years that there has been a cultural awakening. Now there is a lot of German electronic music."

Another difficulty they faced initally was working with drummers. "Our music was always very energetic rhythmically," Hutter says. "We include the body, not just the mind." But drums posed problems in concert. "We always had problems with drummers because they were always banging, and they didn't want to turn electronic. We were working with feedback and tape loops and things and they didn't understand that. Also, ordinary drums are very loud onstage, but past the tenth row you can't hear them. A loudspeaker, on the other hand, you can place anywhere in the room." The solution was to build percussion synthesizers that gave them complete control over the drum sound, and to find musicians who could play these new instruments in a new way — "without a lot of sweating and jumping around."

Two of the four musicians in Kraftwerk are primarily percussionists. Karl Bartos and Wolfgang Flur strike percussion pads with metal sticks, as well as activating and changing the programming on automatic percussion devices. "We built our own drum machines," Hutter points out, "because we were not really pleased with the drum boxes you buy. Some of them are nice, but mostly they sound very Latin. We wanted more machine-like sounds, because that is more what we are about. Our electronic drums are not great inventions or great innovations, but having them has made a strong psychological impact on our performance."

Kraftwerk (which means "power station" in German) first came to the attention of American audiences in 1975, with the release of *Autobahn* (Mercury). The 22-minute title track, with lyrics about riding down the freeway, got some radio airplay in a shortened version. This was the first time they had included vocals in their music. "For nine years," Hutter recalls, "we were afraid to put our voices on tape. We're still paranoid about this, but by now we can handle it." Perhaps partly because of this paranoia, Kraftwerk was one of the first groups to experiment with the vocoder, a device that imprints the pattern of a voice on some other sound and thereby removes the vocalist from the finished sound while leaving the words intact. "When we read that Herbie Hancock was the first to use a vocoder, we laughed, because in Germany we had been doing that for seven or eight years." Of course the vocoder is also a way of making synthesizers and other mechanical sounds sing words, which further blurs the distinction between people and machines.

The success of *Autobahn* led to a series of albums for Capitol Records, which released *Radio-Activity* in 1976, *Trans-Europe Express* in 1977, and *The Man*

"We consider ourselves not so much entertainers as scientists. We work in our studio laboratory, and when we discover something that is true, we put it on tape." —Ralf Hutter

Machine in 1978. But while these records received favorable notice from critics and helped build a cult following for the group, none of them became the kind of runaway sellers that record companies dream about. Following *Man Machine*, Kraftwerk vanished from the scene for three years before re-emerging in 1982 on Warner Brothers with *Computer World*, an album whose theme is the links between people and computers. From a group that had already given us songs with titles like "The Robots," "Spacelab," and "Neon Lights," what could be more natural?

It's an open question how far they can take this image of themselves as robotic, or how serious they are about it. On *Radio-Activity* they sang: "I'm the transmitter, I give information, you're the antenna, catching vibration." On *Trans-Europe Express* the message was: "We are showroom dummies." By the time *Man Machine* came around, it had become: "We are the robots." So it should come as no surprise that the photos of Kraftwerk on the jacket of *Computer World* aren't actually of themselves, but rather a set of life-size mannequins with the musicians' faces. This probably qualifies as self-parody — the technique of consiously overdoing what people who are familiar with your image would expect you to do. But there's a point behind it. As early as 1977 Hutter was speculating: "We are thinking of playing in two cities at the same time. We send some computers to concert halls in different cities. . . ." All they have to do now is animate the mannequins and let *them* play the show.

Which raises an interesting possibility. In the future, if you see Kraftwerk in concert, how will you be able to know for certain whether you're seeing them

COURTESY OF WARENR BROS.

The original Kraftwerk line-up in concert, circa 1970s. Two of the four members (Hutter and Schneider) toured again under the Kraftwerk name in 1998.

or their robots? Hutter would argue, we suspect, that it doesn't matter. "We are not musicians," he explains. "We are musical workers." On another occassion he put it this way: "We consider ourselves not so much entertainers as scientists. We work in our studio laboratory, and when we discover something that is true, we put it on tape." In other words, they conceive of themselves as functional parts of a music-making machine. The functions currently fulfilled by human beings are not necessarily functions that can *only* be filled by human beings. Computer programs for composing music are still in a very primitive stage of development, but there is no reason why future pieces of music, ostensibly by Kraftwerk or by other popular artists, might not be assembled by a computer operating according to parameters programmed into it — or according to parameters it develops on its own.

During the three-year hiatus between *Man Machine* and *Computer World,* Kraftwerk rebuilt all their equipment, with the help of technicians Joachim Dehmann and Gunter Spachtholz, so it could be taken on the road. In fact, what audiences saw during their 1981 tour was the Kling Klang studio itself on stage. "We play studio," Hutter explains, "so we had to take the studio with us. We don't have duplicates of any of our equipment, we have only what we are always working with. It's all in units that break down and go into different cases, and the various components fit together. Some of the components we have are standard things like echo machines, but more than half of the equipment is custom-built by us or with our regular engineers because we couldn't play the music we wanted on regular instruments. We have a couple of standard electronic keyboards, and a small mixing board, and we have digital storage for relatively short-term information, up to six seconds. With this we can store sounds and have them played back rhythmically. Then we have our special electronic percussion systems, which can be programmed for different electronic sounds. We have made up a couple of percussion sounds ourselves, with special circuits. And then we have our singing computer, our synthetic speech machines."

Singing computer? Right. It turns out that some of the mechanical-sounding vocal parts on *Computer World* weren't vocoder at all. The technology already exists for generating computer speech from scratch, and Kraftwerk utilized it in the tune "Numbers" to create a track in which the computer provides the rhythm by counting "one, two, three, four," in various languages. On another tune, a pocket language translator was used. This is a gadget that lets you type in a word and it speaks the word back to you in several languages. (For those of you have the album, the translator is what says, "Business, numbers, money, people" in the title track.) At other times they operate standard EMS vocoders and a customized Sennheiser vocoder, "which Mr Sennheiser built specially for us in the early '70s."

Because the group is so heavily into technology, it's not surprising that they manage to get hold of prototypes of gadgets that aren't being marketed yet. "We call up companies," Hutter says, "and find out about things like special computers that are being used only for office types of things — sales figures, accounting, data storage on people, passport control. We feel that the computers should be used more creatively. And when we hear about things, we step in and try to get them. We have been quite lucky, because the creative people in these companies, the inventors, find great pleasure in talking to other people besides just business people. The inventors have almost a boyish or playful attitude, and they're more open when you call them. Normally, within the big companies, the creative people are always having the marketing people tell them that this will never make it, so they're open to exchanging ideas with creative people from outside."

The 1981 tour also incorporated some small hand-held keyboard instruments made by Casio, the calculator company. The whole band stepped out from behind their consoles to perform at the edge of the stage using these instruments. "This is very liberating for us," Hutter declares. "In the past we have been accused of being boring, because we were always behind the control boards. I don't think the criticism was entirely justified, but certainly there was something to it. But now that we have some things we can walk around with, I think we have broken the barrier of just controlling machines." In addition to the musicians, the Kraftwerk show involves extensive visuals which are put together by Emil Schult, who also gets songwriting credits on some Kraftwerk tunes. The musicians themselves are intensely involved in video, and many of the tunes are conceived of as having both sound and visual elements.

Since most of the better known electronic music — by Wendy Carlos, Larry Fast, and Tomita, for example — is recorded track by track in a laborious process where a single composition may take weeks or even months to complete, it comes as a surprise to find that Kraftwerk records most of their music fairly quickly. "We don't do that many overdubs," Hutter reports, "because our machines are working, and we set everything up simultaneously. Then when we feel that a piece is together, we record it. We go for the total sound at one time. We might add some vocals here or there, but because we work every day in the studio, everything is set up for us; it's like our living room. So once we have the special sound we want, we record it very quickly, because to create it from individual tracks . . . we find that most of the music done on individ-

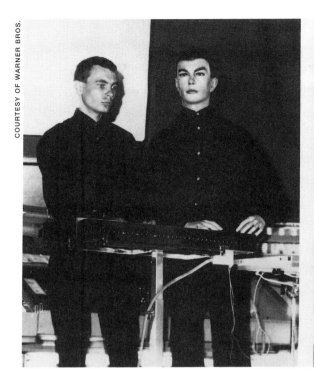

Man and machine: Karl Bartos (L) and Wolfgang Flur

ual tracks gets very boring. It's like when you have a collection of insects and they're walking all over your garden, and then you pick them up individually and sterilize them and stick them to the wall. I think people do that all the time; they break the music apart and record it on 24 or 32 different tracks, and really all the tracks contain nothing. Most of the time we use only ten tracks. Sometimes only two or four tracks." The vocals are recorded on tracks by themselves, however. "We always record the albums in German and then make synchronized versions in English, and some in French, or even Japanese and Italian."

Even in the English versions heard in the United States, however, there will be phrases in other languages. In "The Robots," for example, a voice pronounces a phrase in Russian that Hutter translates as "I'm your servant, I'm your worker." "The word 'robot' actually means 'worker,'" he explains. Along with their message about the unification of man and machine, it seems, Kraftwerk is suggesting that we are all citizens of the same global community. "This is because we live in Dusseldorf," Hutter points out. "It's in Germany, but it's only 20 minutes from Holland and a little more than half an hour from Belgium, not even two hours from France. It's a very mixed area."

The tunes "Europe Endless" and "Trans-Europe Express" also express this idea. "We travel a lot in Europe," Hutter reports. "And it's not like in America, where you travel a thousand miles and you're still in America. Here we have to adapt to different situations more. And electronic music, I find, is by nature an international medium. Radio waves go around the world, and this music can be understood and can communicate with people all around the world. Our music has been called industrial folk music. That's the way we see it. There's something ethnic about it. Wherever you go, you never leave the modern world." This is especially true of Dusseldorf, because the town was the center of German industry before World War ll and consequently was bombed and completely destroyed. The entire city today is newly built. "All our traditions were cut off," Hutter says. "It left a vacuum. We are the first post-War generation, and so we are the beginning of something new."

Because Dusseldorf is still heavily industrial, the sounds of industry have themselves had a direct impact on Kraftwerk's music. "Our first album was recorded in a studio that was right in the middle of an oil refinery," Hutter recalls. "When we came out the door we could hear the sound of those big flames burning off the fumes — all kinds of industrial noises. Even engines are a kind of music. You can hear the harmonics in their tones. When you walk down the street you have a concert; the cars play symphonies. And we use this fact in our music. In 'Autobahn' the cars hum a melody. In 'Trans-Europe Express' the train itself is singing."

But in spite of this emphasis on sound effects, much of Kraftwerk's music has straightforward tonality and simple, easy-to-understand melodic lines. Entire sections of a tune or even whole tunes may be played on a single chord. The music is invariably in 4/4 time, and virtually always falls into precise, regular, four-bar phrases. Which certainly doesn't sound progressive when you describe it that way. The effect on the listener, however, is another story. The regularity of the

"Except for our voices, there is no member of the group producing direct acoustic sounds. We create loudspeaker music." —Ralf Hutter

phrasing and the highly repetitive melodies produce a hypnotic effect. The music always fulfills our most basic subconscious expectations about how a phrase will round out; instead of being jarred by unexpected shifts, we are lulled into a receptive state. This regularity obviously reflects the uniform structure of life in the machine age, but it also calls to mind a pronouncement of Steve Reich, a classical composer who articulated his turn away from the arcane complexities of serial writing toward a simpler, more accessible style by saying: "I don't know any secrets of composition that you can't hear." In other words, like the pipes and girders in a Bauhaus-inspired building, everything in a Kraftwerk tune is out in the open.

The effect of this compositional simplicity is to direct the listener's attention toward the sounds in any given texture — the synthetic percussion, the shimmering background chords, the rich melodic tone colors, and the synthesizer effects. And it is in these sounds themselves and their interlocking rhythmic relationships that Kraftwerk shines. Every tune is a pulsating kaleidoscope of electronic sound. The pulse and phrasing sometimes bring to mind both disco and new wave, but there is a bounciness, and also a kind of restraint or economy, that are vital elements of their style. Generally all the instruments in a mix are clearly audible, and each contributes something specific to the whole. There is no superfluous decoration, any more than there is in an engineer's drawing.

Currently the world of popular music seems to be divided into two camps: those who like electronic sounds, and those who feel that the high-gloss tone of a synthesizer is sterile and lifeless. Even musicians who do use synthesizers sometimes try to disguise the fact. Brian Eno, for example, says that he prefers to subvert the sound of an oscillator by introducing some slight distortion and unevenness, so the result will sound more like an acoustic instrument. But for Kraftwerk, clearly, the synthetic sound is exactly what they want, "Except for our voices," Hutter says, "there is no member of the group producing direct acoustic sounds. We create loudspeaker music." It would be a mistake, though, to assume that their music is entirely devoid of expressive nuance. Their instruments are built to produce warm, rich tones, and there are constant small alterations in timing and tone color that keep the impression from becoming static.

The idea of "creating loudspeaker music" again reflects the pragmatic Bauhaus approach. As somebody else once remarked: "What's this fuss about electronic music? When you listen to a recording of Toscanini conducting Beethoven, you're listening to electronic music." Pretending that you're really hearing Toscanini, and not an amplified electrical signal, is an exercise in self-delusion, an attempt to flee from the reality of living in the future."

In a 1977 interview in *Sounds*, Hutter and Schneider put it this way: "We must move on from the hippie mystical religious stance of the 1960s. The hippies were fugitives from technology. They didn't face the problems, they just ran away. But this is stupid. Wherever you run in the world today, a microphone can pick you up. In the past people said that God could hear everything. Today it is the tape recorder that can hear everything. The tape recorder is the new God."

Certainly this is an extreme view, but it's probably more realistic than most of us would like to admit. Our relationship with our world has been changed forever by technology. The changes in music alone have been immense, and Kraftwerk has documented the changes both in music and in the world at large in a way that few other artists have. The major criticism that might be leveled at them is that at times (as in "Neon Lights" and "Pocket Calculator") they seem to be seduced by the glamour of technology rather than examining its deeper implications. They seem to be paying more attention to surface appearances than to underlying substance. But then, that's a sin of which just about everybody in

"Maybe technology got in the way, so to speak. It was a big advantage, but also learning about it took a lot of energy. I remember a time in Kraftwerk where I just sat around for two-and-a-half years reading manuals, programming a Yamaha DX7 with two Atari computers and two librarians, changing envelopes or whatever, and not making one new composition! This whole fascination with equipment was a thing of the '80s."
—Karl Bartos

this technological culture is guilty. Maybe after all it isn't themselves who Kraftwerk are parodying. Maybe they're parodying us.

[by Jim Aikin, Keyboard, March 1982]

Moving ahead to 1998 . . . original member Karl Bartos departed the fabulous foursome in August '90 to pursue the Elektric Music project — initially in collaboration with Lothar Manteuffel from fellow German group Rheingold. This new recording project was to be called Das Klang Institut (English translation: the Institute of Sound). However, this suitably Teutonic moniker was dropped on account of its sounding too similar to Kraftwerk's infamous

Dusseldorf-based Kling Klang recording studio, where Karl burned the musical midnight oil during the previous 15 years.

Esperanto, Karl's 1993 debut solo offering, was intentionally very Kraftwerk-like; its string sounds are remarkably similar to those heard on the 1976 ground-breaking effort *Radio-Activity.* But its eagerly awaited '98 follow-up, titled simply *Electric Music,* was less synthesized pop and more guitar-driven.

"After *Esperanto,* Bernard [Sumner, of New Order fame] and Johnny [Marr, formerly of The Smiths] came into my life," says Karl, "wanting me to play some percussion tracks on their second Electronic record. I went with them to Manchester, and it turned out to be a two-year project in the end. I've now written nine tracks with them and it's changed my life in a way. The second thing was, I worked with Andy McClusky of OMD, and we did a bit of collaborating on his latest tracks.

"When I worked with Johnny," Karl continues, "he reminded me that I grew up with guitar playing — that I can actually play the guitar. He was a big influence on me because I think he's one of the coolest guitar players around. We became friends and I thought I should make a guitar record — not just a guitar record by putting some guys together playing guitars, but a guitar record using my skills with the computer, with technology, with sampling and sequencing. I wanted to make a real hybrid record, which is probably the main difference. Also, I wasn't just going for so-called techno sounds and structures, but real three-minute pop songs with nice ideas in them. I now have the possibility of reaching people's hearts, whereas with Kraftwerk we reached them intellectually."

Recalling the Kling Klang glory days, Karl laments, "Maybe technology got in the way, so to speak. It was a big advantage, but also learning about it took a lot of energy. I remember a time in Kraftwerk where I just sat around for two-and-a-half years reading manuals, programming a Yamaha DX7 with two Atari computers and two librarians, changing envelopes or whatever, and not making one new composition! This whole fascination with equipment was a thing of the '80s. Back then it was like surgery somehow — electronic boffins on one side, and so-called real musicians on the other! People used to say, 'Those electronic artists can't play. They're just using technology to hide their disabilities.' Like they were missing a limb or something! Now, in the '90s, everything is allowed. There's more crosstalk between musicians from different backgrounds. I mean, I can talk with Johnny Marr about guitars or synths. Separation is a thing of the past. I remember a famous quote of Ralf's: 'The guitar is an instrument from the Middle Ages.' Well, so what? Books date from the middle ages too!"

[by Jonathan Miller, Keyboard, August 1998]

ems synthi a

While most of America's synthesis attention in the late '60s was focused on the creations of Bob Moog and Don Buchla (and soon thereafter, those from ARP), there was only one ballgame to follow in Europe: EMS, makers of the tabletop modular synth called the VCS3, which stood for the voltage-controlled studio, attempt #3, and the Synthi A.

According to Robin Wood, who joined EMS in 1970, "At least half of EMS was a very expensive computer studio where DEC computers were used to control prototype analog systems, not only for generating simple analog synthesizer sounds, but also for some very sophisticated filter bank systems that could analyze sounds. David Cockerell designed this 64-channel analyzing filter bank. It was a bit like a vocoder, only it was all under computer control. The company was heavily into this kind of advanced computer research. There was a group of three of us: Peter Zinovieff, myself, and Tristram Cary.

"The VCS3 was pretty awkward to carry around," says Cockerell. "It would have to be in a box as big as a tea chest. It didn't fold over or anything." But by 1971,

vital stats

Description: One of the first commercially manufactured portable analog synthesizers, conceived by designer David Cockerell and avant-garde composers Tristram Cary and Peter Zinovieff.

Production Dates: 1971-present

Manufacturer: EMS (Electronic Music Studios), United Kingdom.

Approximate Number Made: 850

Original Price: approx. $495

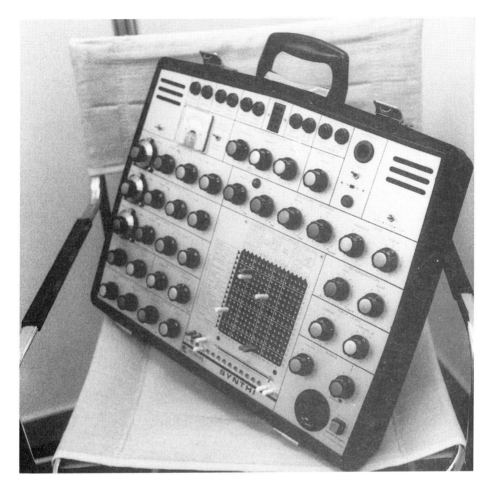

For synthesists
on the go . . .
the EMS Synthi
was Britain's
answer to the
American-made
monoliths of
the time.

Cockerell had squeezed his VCS3 electronics into an oversized briefcase, and the Synthi A was born. He also designed the KS, a 2-1/2-octave touch-plate keyboard with a 256-event monophonic digital sequencer, which fit inside the Synthi A's lid. A combination of the Synthi A and the KS was called the AKS.

Like the American analog synths of the time, EMS's oscillators tended to drift. "They were a bit dodgy onstage," Cockerell reports. "You had to keep tuning them up." Wood concurs, "They're rather temperamental with regard to tuning and pitch stability. People who used them onstage deserve a lot of credit for their bravery. If you wanted to use one with a keyboard in performance, you had to let it settle down for about half an hour before you could set the tuning. Even then, if someone were to open the door and let in cool air just before your lead solo, you could easily be in trouble. Lots of people used them live. Pink Floyd used them for quite a long time. But a lot of their stuff wasn't pitched; it was just effects."

There were several design changes along the way. "The most significant changes came in early '72," Wood explains. "We called them the MkI and MkII. It had a redesigned power supply, which delivered a lot more power in order to drive the KS's monophonic digital sequencer. The original design also used a different output amplifier. On the MkII, you could trigger the envelope using an external audio signal. When the amplifier reached a certain threshold, it triggered the envelope generator, which wasn't possible on the MkIs. The patchboard matrix layout was also slightly changed. On the MkI, there were separate rows for the two oscillator waveforms: sine and sawtooth. You could route the sine wave to, say, ring-modulate some sounds while sending the sawtooth off through the envelope generator to do something else. On the MkII, these were mixed together on one row."

As of 1998, EMS products are still manufactured, sold, serviced, and supported, and have been continuously since 1969. Information can be found online at the Hinton Instruments Web site (www.ems-synthi.demon.co.uk). There's also a modifications page for VCS3/Synthi A on the site at www.hinton. demon.co.uk/ems/emsmods.html.

[by Mark Vail, Keyboard, *November 1990; updates by Greg Rule, 1998*]

Mini-Interviews With Seven Superstars

1 MARILYN MANSON

here are strange days and there are *strange* days, but this one takes the cake.

I'm on a tour bus, face to face with keyboardist Pogo (a.k.a. Madonna Wayne Gacy). He's creepy, very creepy: bald head, piercing eyes, chicken claw dangling from his neck, braided goatee, black leather pants, studded wristbands. We're talking Freddie Krueger/Anton LaVey-grade material here.

It gets weirder. As if interviewing a Lucifer look-alike isn't bizarre enough, two *Hustler* centerfold types enter the bus wearing little more than a smile. They're greeted by Marilyn Manson, singer of the band, who looks like he's just been nailed to the cross — ghostly white, thin as a stick, and covered with what appear to be fresh scars and red makeup. A team of cameramen are in tow, and what happens next is about what you'd expect to happen on a tour bus between a lead singer of decidedly demented appearance and a pair of women who have just stripped off everything but their spike heels. Suffice it to say, this was *not* an average day on the journalistic beat.

Despite the activities, Pogo locks into the interview like a laser beam, completely undistracted by the recreational antics. "I don't consider myself a keyboard

Scary monsters. Marilyn Manson (front) shocked and rocked the music industry like no other in the 1990s. Manson's keyboardist, Madonna Wayne Gacy (a.k.a. Pogo) is the creepy bald guy on the right.

player," he says, rocking back and forth on the couch. "I'm more of a sound de-former. I'll spend hours with the Kurzweil [K2000], not trying to write songs or practice scales or learn chords. I've never been about that . . . I went to school for engineering, I understand computer programming, that's how I got into sampling." And sample he does. Witness the creepy horror-movie textures he contributes to Manson's music (*Portrait of an American Family*, *Smells Like Children*, and *Antichrist Superstar*, all on Nothing Records/Interscope).

Pogo is quick to point out that it's not the gear, but the gear*head* that matters. "You can do amazing things with whatever you have," he stresses. "I've heard people make the most incredible sounds with crappy gear. People come up to me all the time and ask why I'm not sampling in stereo and blah blah blah. I'll sample at a low rate and in mono. Doesn't matter.

"What I do like to do is sample unexpected things," he continues, "like some random thing from a stupid TV commercial. Then I start screwing with it: invert it, take a chunk from its middle and put it at the end, run the whole thing through a filter, mix it with a triangle wave, stick it on tape, run it through some old Morley wah-wah pedal, and sample it back in. I'll fuck it up so bad through filters, distortion, or whatever that it sounds totally unrecognizable."

When it comes to creating creepy sounds, Pogo advises, "It's easy to run to a *Halloween* movie soundtrack or *Nightmare on Elm Street* and get a scary sound, but what's *really* fun is to go back and find something happy — *H.R. Puffenstuff* or some toy commercial — get a sound out of that and twist it into the most evil, horrifying thing in the world." Coming from the most evil, horrifying keyboardist in the world, we'll gladly heed his advice.

[by Greg Rule, Keyboard, January 1996]

② JUAN ATKINS

back in June 1982, *Keyboard* magazine published a cover story on something called "the new synthesizer rock." Artists like Depeche Mode, Gary Numan, Soft Cell, and OMD were stripping rhythm down to the basics and playing sparse synth lines in chilly timbres. Vocals in these bands hovered in the baritone depths, a league or two below Jon Anderson's boy soprano range. The whole thing sounded kind of grim, but at least it was fresh, and perhaps as much of a tonic to what had preceded it as punk was to shred guitar.

Important as the story was, we didn't understand how big it would become within just a few years. We noted the influence of disco on these acts, but what we didn't know was that funk and synth-based new music were already finding common ground somewhere outside of Detroit. There, a teenager named Juan Atkins was puzzling out ways of infusing electronic music with the kind of energy that dance-oriented R&B bands generated with real-time musicians. Along with a friend named Rick Davis, who called himself 3070, Atkins formed Cybotron, a duo dedicated to amplifying the ideas of Alvin Toffler and other futurist writers through music. Later, expanded to a threesome with Jon-5, they put out a collection of tunes that Fantasy later released on the album *Clear*.

Considered the "Godfather of Techno" by many, Juan Atkins defied Motown trends in late '70s and put synth music on the Western map.

These early works borrowed heavily from European techno-pop, especially Kraftwerk; the title track on *Clear* echoes a string synth motif from "Trans-Europe Express." But over time, through working with different collaborators and growing more sophisticated with the tools of his trade, Atkins developed a more original vision. His tempos sped up, with intricate interplay between elements of the rhythm track and the synth. As early as the mid-'80s, Atkins was using sounds familiar to Soft Cell fans in instrumental works that stretched far beyond traditional structure: Recording under the name Model 500, he cut "The Chase" in '86, with percussion and comp parts adding a funky feel never explored by British synthesists

Even earlier, in '85, his "No UFOs" used the kind of high-register syncopated figure, quick bass drum kicks, and minor-mode theme — $B\flat$-E-$D\flat$, over an $E\flat$ minor chord — that defined the sound soon known to the world as techno.

In any number of ways, techno revolutionized pop music. It brought the do-it-yourself ethic of studio-based synth music down to the trenches and offered young artists an alternative to garage bands. Like punk and other high-energy movements, it came up from the clubs, not down from record label boardrooms. It permutated quickly; when Atkins took "No UFOs" to Chicago's Powerplant, along with his Roland TR-909, DJ Frankie Knuckles picked up on his energy and helped launch the house music movement. Tapes by Cybotron, Model 500, and other Detroit artists — Derrick May, Kevin Saunderson, Kenny Larkin — became a launching pad for ambient house, deep house, and myriad other machine-based dance/trance styles. Though each of these variations is distinct, all are connected to the ideas pioneered by Atkins some 15 years ago. Yet, as an aftereffect of techno's alternative roots, he is little-known to people outside the industry. It's not easy to find Atkins's material. Although he does have vinyl singles and EPs available on his Metroplex label, nothing is out under his own name at this time, and much of what he's working on now isn't intended for U.S. release. *[Ed. Note: TVT Records released an Atkins CD in 1998.]* Even as techno spreads and dilutes across the face of mainstream music, echoes of Atkins's techno innovations embedded themselves into the cultural consciousness of our time.

How would you explain techno music to musicians from a more traditional orientation?

Maybe the best way to address that would be to say that this whole movement started as the techno — short for "technology" — movement. That says that technology, within the past ten years, has enabled a lot of people to make music who maybe ten years ago would not have been able to. It's not a bad thing, because music is sound. If something sounds pleasing to the ear, then what does it matter how much technical skill the person has who produced the sound? If it touches you, then the technical skill doesn't matter.

Did you listen much to the early popular synthesists, like Wendy Carlos?

Yeah, and Isao Tomita, Synergy [Larry Fast], stuff like that. It was interesting but, for me, kind of in the background. I didn't pay too much attention to it, but because I was into electronics I was cognizant of it.

Were you listening to people like Soft Cell, the Human League, and early Depeche Mode?

Yeah, I listened to that. Devo, B-52s. Even Grace Jones: "Warm Leatherette," "Love Is a Drug," stuff like that. Of course, P-Funk Stevie Wonder, to a certain degree. James Brown. These people used music technology to very different degrees. Yeah. Even Funkadelic, in the early days, didn't have a lot of technology. The synthesizer didn't come in until the stuff they started making after '75.

Was Kraftwerk a big influence?

I had already been experimenting and dabbling with the synthesizer before I heard Kraftwerk. The funny thing about it was that when I heard them, they were using some of the same sounds I had been making on the Korg MS-10. It made me freeze in my tracks. Coming from Germany, these guys were like a world away. In fact, at that time, it was almost like coming from another planet. But they were using the same sounds I was. And they were so precise! I didn't really have any knowledge of sequencers at that time. I was barely grasping the synthesizer, so I didn't have any clue about the concept of sequencing. I had read certain things about sequencers, but they were never in laymen's terms to tell you exactly what they did. So when I heard Kraftwerk, of course that's what they were using, but I didn't know how they were making these notes so precise. My thing was really raggedy by comparison. I didn't have the ability to make my notes fall precisely where they were supposed to fall. It was electronic and it was weird, but nothing was too precise. Of course, you wanted to do something different with your groove than they were doing with theirs. Yeah. I had my funk and dance thing.

You mentioned the Korg MS-10. How did you use it?

I'd ping-pong stuff with two Kenwood cassette machines and a little Yamaha mixer. I'd just do overdubs.

What drew you to that synth?

It was the idea of being able to create sounds that had not existed. Since I was kind of spacey anyway and into science fiction, it was the perfect thing for me. I was always into spaceships landing and taking off. When the synthesizer came, it put those imagined sounds into reality. . . . I was into synthesis before presets. I never could accept using the presets. I mean, I'm a synthesist. The whole concept behind that is to synthesize sounds. If you're just going to punch up a preset, you're not really synthesizing.

While all this was happening, you were going to Belleville High School with two other important techno pioneers, Derrick May and Kevin Saunderson.

Yeah. Derrick is a year younger than me, and Kevin is two or three years younger. But I made my first record in '81, and Derrick didn't make his first record until '87. When I graduated from high school, I went directly to community college, and that's where I met Rick Davis. He bridged the gap of knowledge I needed about sequencers because he was really advanced in that area. He already had a couple of sequencers and a roomful of synthesizers. All I had was this little MS-10.

What kind of gear did he have?

He had an ARP Odyssey, an ARP Axxe, the first Roland sequencer, and the Roland RS-09 string machine. At that point, though, Rick was really isolated. This was a time when everybody was still wanting to get together and jam. The disco thing was going out and R&B was coming in. It felt stale. But Rick had mastered the art of doing his own demos, so when he heard one of my tapes he invited me over. We got together, came up with Cybotron, and did our first record, "Alleys of Your Mind," which we released on our own label.

You went on to release dozens of important records under names such as Channel One and Model 500. Today, how do you feel about the impact techno has made on Europe?

It kind of came out of left field. I mean, now those places in Europe don't seem that far away because I've been there so many times. But at the time it started happening, it seemed so far removed that I couldn't even anticipate that kind of reaction, so it was definitely a pleasant surprise.

What's your take on all the permutations of techno that have come down over the past ten years — ambient, acid, trance, and so on?

That's a result of the U.K. They tend to be kind of trendy, and I don't mean that in a bad way. They're always looking for something to move on to. One thing about the U.K. is the people there are more open-minded than anywhere else toward anything new or innovative. That constant appetite for different things, for the next trend, is something I can relate to.

[by Robert L. Doerschuk, Keyboard, July 1995]

③ PHOTEK

he's been electrifying Europe for years with his edge-cutting drum 'n' bass work, but over across the Atlantic, Photek is just getting plugged in.

Hailing from St. Alban's, England, Rupert Parkes (his real name) has released half a dozen 12" records on his own label over the past five years, but until recently the only one to hit the States was the critically acclaimed *Hidden Camera* EP. His style, adequately summed up in his bio, is "a combination of '70s jazz fusion, Detroit techno, and unscored film music."

Photek's low profile in the States is about to change. He's been featured on MTV's *Amp* and companion CD, and even more exciting for jungle-heads, his full-length release on Astralwerks *Modus Operandi* is taking off. "Out of the 11 tracks [on *Modus*], three were previously released," he says. "But everything else is new."

Rupert's tracks are a lesson in intricacy, and he takes his sweet time realizing them. "I work at home most of the time," he explains, "and it's best 'cause I spend such a long time on my tunes. Since the past year and a half, the pace that I work at has slowed down 'cause I spend a lot of time away from the

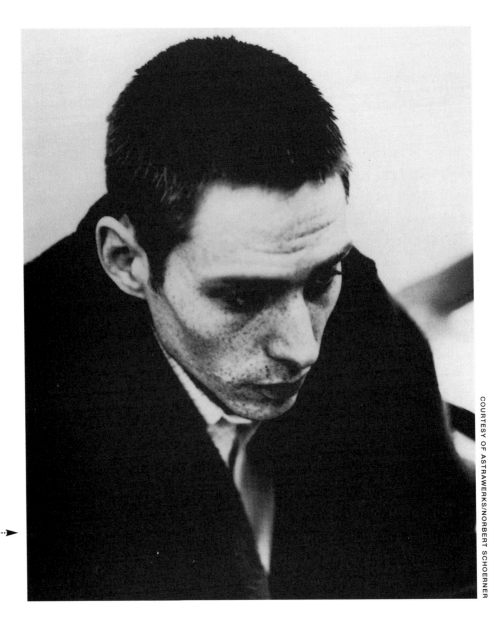

Drum 'n' bass
pioneer Rupert
Parkes (a.k.a.
Photek).

studio just thinking about what I'm going to do next. The way I'm working at the moment . . . I'd say five weeks, minimum, to complete a track. And that's the reason my music sounds like it does, because I don't care how much time I'm putting into what I'm doing. That's the way I've always treated it."

In his home studio, Rupert uses a surprisingly sparse setup. "The only equipment I use is just the usual." He has an E-mu E4 and e64, Cubase on the PC, "and various outboard effects. Sometimes I'll use a module like the Roland JV-1080, but quite often I'll use the less distinctive sound. I'll find a nothing-in-particular sound, and then work with filters, effects, and EQ to give it some character. I might put a highpass filter envelope on the hi-hats, for example."

Speaking of hi-hats, Rupert's beats are among the best in the biz. His secret? "Well, the thing about the beats is. . . . Like 'Photek #6,' I don't sample any breakbeats off records, and that's why it takes me so long to make tunes. I'm programming like you would on an 808 drum machine by sampling, like, a couple of snare drums and a few hi-hats, and just programming them in. The trick is crafting a drum program into sounding like an old R&B break. That's what I'm trying to do, and that's what takes so long. I'm not lifting loops off any records — I'm programming from scratch."

He'll often grab sounds off vinyl, "but because I break them down to such small molecules, like a hi-hat, there's no rhythmic content in my samples. And the source can be anything. So sometimes I'll go to a studio and do one big session. Last year I sampled a drum kit, and I did, like, 50 snare drums at different velocities and different areas. And then I did the same with all the cymbals and drums, so I have a stock of flatly EQ'd drum samples. I sample CDs sometimes too."

Drums aren't the only live instruments he samples in the studio. Upright and electric basses are also targets of his microphone. "I've got a few DATs from sessions I've done where I had bass players come in and play all up and down the scale, and at different strengths so you get the strings buzzing and all that. Then I'll use EQ to make them sound different." Those sounds eventually get poured into his E-mu samplers, "but if I sample something raw," he cautions, "very rarely will it sound like that on the record. I do a lot of strange EQ, and things like playing it a few octaves away from the original. I mean, sometimes I might make up a multisample so I can play up and down [the key range], but I do like to take specific notes and play them like I do with the drums — shifted up or down a couple octaves."

Except for the occasional offsite sampling session, everything Photek does to a track is accomplished at home. Including mixdown. However, "I never really sit and *mix* a track," he confides. "I mean, I'll work on it, and adjust it to sound right as it's developing. Then, once I reach a point where I think it's done, I'll record it straight to DAT." His near-field monitors of choice are Soundcraft Absolute 2s, "and a lot of the time I'll just work on Sennheiser headphones. But I think it's more a question of time and experience to get a good mix."

If you're anxious to catch Photek in concert anytime soon, don't hold your breath. "I don't think the live thing is something I'm ever going to get into," he concludes. "Because of the way I work, I don't really see playing live as something that makes sense. It's such a laborious process in the studio, and it's so controlled, that to make that happen on the spur of the moment, after it took five weeks, is too unlikely."

[by Greg Rule, Keyboard, November 1997]

4 KMFDM

*L*et's clear one thing up, right here, right now. Contrary to popular belief, KMFDM does not stand for Kill Mother F—ing Depeche Mode. Sorry, Mode haters. It's actually a German acronym for "Kein Mehrheit für die Mitleid," which roughly translates to "no pity for the majority."

Since the late '70s, KMFDM has been true to their acronym. Fist-in-the-air, head-in-the-speakers industrial-techno-metal isn't exactly the stuff of pop radio or MTV playlists. But the revolving collective, anchored by Sascha Konietzko, has produced nine high-impact records that have earned them a large, loyal fanbase strewn across the planet.

Released in 1997, the band's unpronounceable 5-symbol CD on TVT/Wax Trax was an all-star affair, teaming Konietzko and core members En Esch and Gunter Schulz with Tim Skold (Skold), Ogre (Skinny Puppy), Raymond Watts (Pig), Abby Travis (Beck, Elastica), William Rieflin (Ministry, Rev Co), and Michel Bassin (Treponem Pal). Don't look for any secret meaning in the CD's title. "No message," says Sascha about the symbols. "It's just . . . that was one of the first ideas for a KMFDM album title that we ever had, before we even had an album out. But then the idea got lost for years."

KMFDM master-
minds Sascha
Konietzko (L)
and En Esch.
One of the most
prolific industrial
bands in history,
KMFDM called
it quits in late
1998. Their final
CD was *Adios* on
TVT/Wax Trax.

You've been at this for over 20 years. Are you still as buzzed today making records as you were in the beginning?

Probably even more. The experience sort of re-establishes itself every time. I mean, in the beginning it was more, "Yeah, whatever. I don't really know why we're doing this, but we're doing it anyway." Now we know damn well why we're doing it.

How did the making of the new record differ from making 1996's *XTort* ?

The difference was the approach. I started *XTort* after coming off two pretty extensive tours in '95. What I did was, I sat down and totally re-did my studio. I switched all my sampling stuff from [E-mu] Emax II to Akai [samplers], I started using the Doepfer MS-404, and various kinds of things. I ended up spending a lot of time working with Gunter [Schulz] and F.M. Einheit; working without a real musical direction in mind, but more like, "What can we do now?" And so on this last record, everyone came to Seattle for a couple weeks, and we just started recording. Everybody put in as much stuff as they had, and then afterwards we sorted through all the stuff and assigned everyone a couple of things — a couple of tracks or rough ideas. Then everybody went back into their own studios and started working. They came back to Seattle frequently, and we worked together and developed the whole thing. So at some point we had about 17 tracks that were all potentially going to be overdubbed on, sung on, and so forth.

They were all instrumentals at that point?

All instrumentals with rough sketchings on guitar, and rough vocal ideas sometimes. Then we got together for a month, started overdubbing and mixing. And then the whole Jaz drive scenario happened when we were trying to mix the first version of the album. My idea was to drop everything that was in the computer, audio-wise, onto formats like ADATs and 24-track tape, and then use the computer timecode-locked to mix the tracks down. So basically, the mixes can be edited with a quantized cursor and that kind of stuff. And in order to store the massive amounts of data mix after mix after mix — you know, vocal only, guitar up, guitar down, and all that kind of stuff — we figured we needed good, fast, reliable storage media cheap. And that's when the Jaz drive scenario came into play. At that point, there were a couple of people I'd worked with who said, "Oh, yeah. Jaz drives are doing miraculously well for us." They weren't all audio people, though, mostly graphics and video. [*Ed. Note: To make a long story short, the Jaz data was corrupted. Sascha and company lost all of their mixes and had to start over.*]

This record turned out to be less guitar-intensive than previous efforts. You're quoted in the bio as saying: "Personally, I was tired of having to deal with a barrage of guitars and having no room for any other frequencies coming through. We wanted the guitars to be more of an accompaniment and less of a driving force throughout the record."

Historically, *Angst* is my least favorite KMFDM record. It was done in an almost similar fashion, where we all sat down in the beginning and started

> ## "The experience [of making records] sort of re-establishes itself every time. I mean, in the beginning it was more, Yeah, whatever. I don't really know why we're doing this, but we're doing it anyway. Now we know damn well why we're doing it."

writing material, but we had two guitarists. Every song was really centered around guitar riffs, and in the end, the stuff became so massive there was hardly any room for other instruments to get through it. So ever since then, I've tried to work on the balance between having a lot of guitars yet at the same time really letting my kind of stuff come through a little more. I think *XTort* and this album are definitely steps in that direction.

Having done the record modularly, where data was shuttled around to various home studios, do you think you'd do it again that way in the future?

Yeah. I would absolutely do it again. It worked really well. You don't get the aggravation of hanging together all the time, and you don't have to compromise so much. I think the first draft of this album suffered most from too many cooks. One guy would say "kick up" and the next guy would say "kick down." One guy would say "more compression" next guy would say "less compression." So in the end it stayed like it was, which wasn't so good.

Over the past couple of years, electronica has started to gain momentum in the States. Did that influence you at all during the making of this record?

Not really. First of all, I don't pay that much attention to what's going on in, like, the pages of *Rolling Stone* magazine or things like that. In terms of general acceptance, though, yeah, I think it was a good thing. Surprisingly so. I think what struck me at first the most was that Gunter and En Esch's input was so "electronica driven," so to speak. I must say, too, that Gunter and En Esch recently started using computers and sequencing — really getting into the technological world. Up to that point it was mostly myself doing that stuff. And they came up with good stuff, contemporary and futuristic. I can't stress this enough: The initial phase of brainstorming and putting things together was really the main maker of this record, regardless of however many changes the stuff went through afterwards. That was key.

Your gear list is extensive. Are there any particular pieces that were essential to the sound of this record?

The [Doepfer] MS-404 is definitely one of my favorite boxes 'cause it's just so handy. Send it any sort of MIDI triggers, and it just goes on and on. When I'm doing the initial programming for bass and so on, I'm finding myself more and more using the [Clavia] Nord Lead. It's so handy when it comes to syncing the arpeggiator and those kinds of things. I would say that a good part of it is vintage synths, like mainly the [Sequential] Pro One and [Korg] Mono/Poly. Other than that, it's mostly studio hardware. Everything goes through Manley compressors and Neve 1081s, and that really defines most of the sound. I've got my favorite settings on the Manleys that I hardly ever change, and everything pumps right through it.

What settings are those?

With the compressors, I look for a fast release, fast attack, and medium threshold, so you don't really suck out too much of the low end, but it still gives punch. It really pulls everything together, especially when you work with strange loops, like everything Bill would come up with . . . stuff that was recorded with a [Shure] SM58, mono, on a portable DAT channel or something. I would, for example take that, copy it, and then run the whole thing through an [Eventide] H3000, harmonize each side up eight or nine cents, and compress it. But they're just the tiniest bit off and stereoized. A lot of the stuff I've been shooting for is making three-dimensional or stereo-type images. Like, I'd always go for a stereo bass, even though it might not be totally obvious. But it comes from both sides and hits you right in the chest.

*[by Greg Rule, **Keyboard, May 1998]***

⑤ FRANKIE KNUCKLES

With "disco sucks" emblazoned on every other T-shirt and car bumper in the early '80s, a core group of DJs, producers, and musicians bucked the trend and put dance music back on the map. Named for the Warehouse nightclub where Frankie Knuckles spun his way into history, house music took disco to the next level. Diva vocals and four-on-the-floor kicks survived the name change, but many of disco's live drum, bass, and horn lines gave way to drum-machine- and synth-based tracks. "And when we couldn't get that feel with drum machines," says star DJ/producer Farley "Jackmaster" Funk, "then we'd *sample* disco."

In addition to Frankie, Farley, and Jesse Saunders, pioneers such as Adonis, Tyree Cooper, Jeff Davis, Chip E., Ron Hardy, Andre Hatchett, Steve "Silk" Hurley, Marshall Jefferson, DJ Pierre, Jamie Principle, Ten City, and Wayne Williams (to name a few) all played historic roles in taking house from a small club to the world. Many of the above are featured on *Chicago Reunion*, a double-CD compilation on Jesse Saunders' Broken Records label.

Frankie Knuckles and the Warehouse nightclub were to Chicago House what the Grateful Dead and Haight-Ashbury were to the San Francisco psychedelic

The origin of "house" music can be traced to the late 1970s in Chicago, where DJ/remixer Frankie Knuckles held court at the Warehouse after-hours club. Frankie won the first-ever Remixer of the Year Grammy in 1998.

scene. Chicago was the birthplace of the genre, and Frankie was smack dab in the heart of it. "When I moved to Chicago in '77," he tells us, "I was playing a lot of the Philly soul stuff, and disco was really big at that point. At the time, Chicago didn't have any other after-hours clubs like the Warehouse. The Warehouse was a lot like the Garage [in New York City] — a big after-hours club, no alcohol. It was a three-story building [located at 206 S. Jefferson Street in downtown

> **"The single most important instrument that signified the house sound, in my opinion, was and is the Roland [TR-] 909. It set the standard at the time, and it's still being used. It's pretty much a staple in what we do [today] at Def Mix." —Frankie Knuckles**

Chicago]. One floor was dedicated solely to the dance floor, one was a lounge, and the bottom floor was another lounge with a kitchen. It was a lot like being in someone's house."

Disco was still booming in '77, but mainstream perceptions changed a few years later. "When all those people claimed that disco was dead, it didn't really affect me at the Warehouse, except that there weren't too many disco or dance records being put out anymore. You either had down-tempo, heavy soul or country-western." But perhaps it was a blessing in disguise because the disco drought motivated Frankie to start remixing tracks. "I found myself having to rely on fewer records, and if I liked them, I had to completely re-edit them, or rework them to make them work on my dance floor. There were records coming out that were okay, but they just didn't have enough punch to get my dance floor interested."

With tape and a razor blade, Frankie started splicing together new versions of songs in 1979, strategically cutting in breakbeats from other records. Lo-fi, yet very effective. "Frankie was phenomenal with that tape stuff," says Farley "Jackmaster" Funk. And the Warehouse wasn't the only club to hear Frankie's custom tracks; he took the tapes on tour with him as well, fast gaining recognition for his custom mixes.

Frankie would soon raise his productions to the next level, incorporating original synth and drum machine tracks. "The single most important instrument that signified the house sound, in my opinion, was and is the Roland [TR-] 909. It set the standard at the time, and it's still being used. It's pretty much a staple in what I do at Def Mix, working with Satoshi [Tomiie], David [Morales], and Terry Burris."

Speaking of Def Mix, Frankie says the team now has its system down to a science. "It's great, because having worked with them for so many years, they pretty much know me. Satoshi has tagged all these sounds in the library that are my sounds, so if it's gonna be a writing day, for example, he knows exactly what to go for, and he'll have everything up and ready for when I get there. These days, to get the basic tracks down, it usually only takes us a couple of hours."

As producer, songwriter, and remixer, Frankie's discography reads like a *Who's Who*: Michael Jackson, Elton John, Neville Brothers, Diana Ross, Toni Braxton, Quincy Jones, Chaka Khan, En Vogue, Lisa Stansfield, Patti LaBelle, Ace Of Base, Janet Jackson, Luther Vandross, Pet Shop Boys, and on and on. Be on the lookout for his work on *Blood on the Dancefloor*, a new remix CD of Michael Jackson classics. Frankie won the first ever "Remixer of the Year" grammy in 1998.

Even though Frankie Knuckles is one of the most sought-after dance producer/remixers on the planet, he still has his heart in clubland. "The club is paramount," he stresses. "Without that forum, it would be very difficult for me to write the kind of music that I do. Being able to test it on the dance floor . . . that's the one thing I really get off on: turning the audience on to something new that I've done."

Comparing the past to the present, he has encouraging news for start-up dance music artists. "With technology, anybody can set up a studio in their house now, and do it all from there. A lot of these dance records coming out today are done by bedroom producers. But back then, it was all different. I didn't have the technology, for one. I had a razor blade, a Pioneer reel-to-reel, and spools and spools of recording tape."

Today the Warehouse is long gone, but the music it birthed still fuels dance floors across the planet. And like other established genres, house has spawned a family of sub-styles: deep house, hip-house, acid house, garage, handbag . . . the list goes on.

[by Greg Rule, Keyboard, August 1997]

⑥ ARMAND VAN HELDEN

While the American mainstream is learning who's who on the electronic dance front, Armand Van Helden is living large. Still in his 20s, he's become a bonafide superstar — raking in bucks and fans all over the planet. His early dance singles "Witchdoktor" and "Funk Phenomenon" set the stage, but his monster remixes for the likes of Tori Amos and the Sneaker Pimps really catapulted Armand to the top of the heap.

In 1997 he remixed the cream of the crop: Janet Jackson's "Got 'Til It's Gone," the Rolling Stones' "Anybody Seen My Baby," Sneaker Pimps' "Spin Spin Sugar," Daft Punk's "Around the World," and Sean "Puffy" Combs' "It's All About the Benjamins." As a result, and rightly so, he was nominated for the first-ever "Remixer of the Year" Grammy award.

But Armand isn't just remixing, he's producing his own material as well. He hopes to grab a firm foothold on the charts as a solo artist with his full-length debut on RuffHouse/Columbia, *Enter the Meat Market*, a collection of original old-school-style hip-hop tracks. A second solo album of house tracks is already in the works.

COURTESY OF RUFF HOUSE RECORDS/COLUMBIA/PAULINE ST. DENIS

Armand Van Helden, one of the most respected (and highest-paid) remixers of the 1990s.

When you sample, what's your primary source material? Vinyl?

Everything I get, all my source stuff, is from diggin' in my [record] crates. Every single track I do.

How much editing do you do to your samples?

It depends. Now, like in hip-hop, you can just loop Steely Dan and make the biggest record. That's happening right now. Hip-hop's easy. If you get the right loop, like all the Premieres and Puffys of the world, it's worth gold. But it's *getting* that right loop, and it's what you do to it. What I'm saying is in all the other stuff I do, like in the house stuff and these type of things, I don't loop hardly anything [opting to sequence note-for-note]. The only loops I have are at the end of a song to make an effect.

Tell us about your "Spin Spin Sugar" remix.

Well, it's funny about that one. When it came in, I didn't know who the Sneaker Pimps were. You know, this is the life I live in New York. I don't know much about alternative groups. I didn't know who Tori Amos was either. I didn't even know who the Spice Girls were until six months ago. So you understand, I live a very urban life. But my manager asked me about it, and I got a cassette. That's how it started.

And the Sneaker Pimps hadn't really broken through in the States at that point.

No, they hadn't hit anywhere, so it wasn't a priority at all. But I finally sat down with the cassette and peeped it out. And I said, "Ya know what, this could probably work. This is half speed of house. I could put a house beat right over this." Her vocal was like 60, 62, or maybe 64 bpm. Real slow. But if you double it, it's 128.

So you didn't have to time-stretch?

I didn't have to do anything, which was good. So, as soon as I got the DAT from Virgin, I put the whole a cappella in [Opcode] Studio Vision, and when I put a beat over it I got chills. I'm like, "This is going to be nasty! This is going to be dope."

Describe how you built this remix.

The thing to remember, with me, everything you hear in that mix is a sample. I'm talking everything! There's no loops. Here's my process: When I do a mix, I'll put the a cappella in the computer, I'll set the bpm, and just put a simple beat in. I can take any kick and snare, lock it tight, and that's where I start. From there I go to my Roland [S-]760 and I literally fill that thing up with samples in a matter of an hour and a half. I've got about a 100-seconds stereo in it, and I just fill it up with mad beats, bass, notes, stabs, whatever quirky little sounds. Everything that's in my mixes comes from someplace else. I love the art of sampling. You can listen to "Spin Spin Sugar" and never know where I got anything from. That's the art of it. Drum 'n' bass is based on that. That's where that shit comes from. All the stuff that Roni Size does, which is musically now so respected, is a sample.

So even that big bass line in your "Spin Spin Sugar" remix was a sample?

"We have a 'no recall' policy, and this is a new thing in remixing. It's not to dis, but back in the days when Picasso was hired to do a painting, he painted it. You either liked it or you didn't, but you paid for it and took it. That's how it worked. Now that's how it works with me. 'Armand, what he does is art. Respect what he does. You want a mix from him, there's no recall.'"

Yeah. But actually that bass came from their DAT. And that's another thing, see, like with the Tori Amos [remix] too, that bass was from her bassist or whoever was in her band. So it all depends on what I get on DAT. In the Sneaker Pimps case, I had a five-minute track of bass, and I just grabbed that one little thing off it.

Are you often asked to change things after you've submitted a mix?

The way me and my manager have it set up is, we have a "no recall" policy, and this is a new thing in remixing. It's not to dis. It's not to point anyone out. But back in the days when Picasso was hired to do a painting, he painted it. You either liked it or you didn't, but you paid for it and took it. That's how it worked. Now that's how it works with me. "Armand, what he does is art. Respect what he does. You want a mix from him, there's no recall. That's how it works." We're the only people doing that, though, because the label or the artist always wants to be a part of it. It's not to disrespect them, but we're trying to put remixing in a place where it needs to be.

Are you still getting flat fees, or are you getting into points now?

Flat fee. And it's because the amount of time and phone calls you have to put in to collect your points is a nightmare. Even for an artist signed to a label; it's a nightmare. They [the record labels] will hold out 'til the very last minute, until you're about to sue them. And it's just a fucking game that all the labels play. It's a part of major label business. Their whole thing is, "Don't sweat nothing until the dire last minute — until we're about to go to court." That's how they work. So me and my manager finally said, "Fuck all this drama trying to get paid! Let's just set the rate high to compensate, and just get it flat."

Some people might argue that a flat fee could be a rip-off to an artist whose remix hits big.

My Tori Amos remix blew up, and you know what, I didn't see nothing from that. Zero. But at the same time I got about 40,000 other mixes because of it. You see what I'm saying? So, in a way I did get paid back from it. And probably easier and faster than trying to collect it from the label.

Word on the street is that you pull in anywhere from 25 to 50 grand per mix. Is that true?

Yeah, but again, a lot of it's my manager 'cause I really don't do any of the talking. The whole thing started out last year. I was doing mixes at that time for about $25,000. And that's high, but that's pretty much what the best people were getting. But what happened was, I wanted to do a hip-hop album, and I said, "I don't want do any remixes. Set the price crazy high so nobody will bite." And people bit. So, we were like, "If they're going to bite at $30,000, lets go to 35. And then if they're gonna bite at 35, let's go to 40." And that's how it ended up. It's just business. You know? I mean, you create a demand, and if you're turning in quality stuff, you jack the price.

*[by Greg Rule, **Keyboard,** June 1998]*

7 JOSH WINK

much of today's breakthrough dance music emanates from other continents, but the U.S. is gaining momentum thanks to artists like the Crystal Method, Armand Van Helden, and, the subject of this profile, Josh Wink.

Wink is a world-class dance-music artist, producer, remixer, DJ, and co-founder of Ovum Recordings (a Ruffhouse/Columbia affiliate). European club-goers know him well. He's topped their charts with club anthems "Higher State of Consciousness," "Don't Laugh," and "I'm Ready," but he's breaking through in the States thanks to *Herehear*, his first full-length for Ovum. *Herehear* is an eclectic electronic affair that finds Wink mixing it up with an all-star supporting cast, including Trent Reznor. The mood swings from numbing ambient and trance tracks to energetic jungle and edgy electro-pop songs.

"The first half of the record is little more intellectual," says Wink, "more thought-provoking. The second half is a little more dancy, techno-based. The way I work is ever-changing, and that's the thing. Being an electronic musician, and being a DJ, I get bombarded with all this new cool music, and it

Josh Wink's
eclectic, elec-
tronic full-length
debut, Herehear,
was released
in 1998 on
Ovum/Columbia.
Wink co-founded
the Ovum label.

influences me in a sense to make a certain kind of music. Not to imitate, but to be influenced by."

Did you have a blueprint in mind when you set out to make *Herehear*?

It originally started with the idea of doing an album based on textures; textures as in visually, how you would see them, and also how they were heard. But the album changed. It's kinda like asking an artist how they go in and start a painting, or asking a musician how they go in and start a track. For me, the first step was getting in the studio. Let me just say that I've changed as an artist. I used to be a singles-driven artist. I used to make singles, one-off records for different labels throughout the world, and that was that. But when certain songs started blowing up worldwide, the label wanted me to do an album. "Okay, I'll do an album." And then I thought, "Wow, people aren't just going to be listening to my music in clubs anymore. They could be listening to it at home while they do the dishes, clean house, whatever." So all of a sudden I started thinking of a whole new audience — the at-home audience, the recliner audience. This was something new for me. And so this album is eclectic as a result.

Take us inside the studio with you as you were creating the new songs. Did you generally start with, say, a drum loop or bass line?

When I make dance music, I think of the audience, the crowd, and I think of how they would react. My music, basically, is built around tension. I love the tension in music in terms of build-ups and climaxes, and if it's gonna happen or if it's not gonna happen. And a lot of that is used when I DJ too. As a DJ, someone who makes music out of pre-existing music, I use effects to. . . . Some DJ mixers have effects built in, some have EQ where you can take out all the bass or tweak the treble, and really make a new track by blending and shaping things. And so I love to do this sort of thing. I try to take that approach in a lot of my own dance tracks.

And yet you're stretching into less dance-intensive areas as well.

That's my eclecticism and diversity — being raised with an open mind. I like a little bit of everything, and I think it shows on this album. I don't necessarily know how or why I lean toward different things. It's not like I go into the studio and say, "Today I'm going to make an ambient track." And even if I did, I can guarantee you it's not always gonna turn out to be an ambient track. It may turn out to be a hip-hop track, or a drum 'n' bass track, or a techno track, or a house track, or a rock track. The steps I take in the studio depend upon the type of music I'm making, and my mood, which dictates the tempo.

I have something that I work under called the mistake theory, which is: I use a lot of things that you and I might consider mistakes. By screwing around with effects, with filters, with percentages in my sampler, and just doing unconventional stuff that you wouldn't ordinarily do. If I have a perfect loop, I might take it down another fifth. You accidentally hit something with your elbow, or the power goes off and things come back on with weird settings. This is what I call the mistake

"When I make dance music, I think of the audience, the crowd, and I think of how they would react. My music, basically, is built around tension. I love the tension in music in terms of build-ups and climaxes, and if it's gonna happen or if it's not gonna happen."

theory, and I try to do it now with almost everything. Right now I'm working on a series of stuff, from experimental techno and house to an entire project based on just a straight sine tone. The rhythms, beats, the pulsing sounds are all coming from a straight sine tone, and the mistake theory worked well with that because the stuff is completely minimal. It mean, it's not all just tone; there are percussive elements in it. Lots of driving rhythms, but it's very sparse. I've only done two tracks of it so far, but I'm getting so much out of this minimal approach.

You brought in some interesting artists for this record: Ursula Rucker, Caroline Crawley, the Interpreters, and Trent Reznor. How did the collaboration with Trent happen?

That actually happened through Jason Jordan, who does A&R for Columbia and Ovum. I sent a couple of tapes out to people who I hoped to get vocals from. So I sent Trent a tape, and I heard back that he was interested, and that he wanted to do something with it. We talked several times on the phone, I talked with his whole crew down in New Orleans. It turned out really well. His writing really complemented it. You heard the track; it's a weird track. I mean, you wouldn't expect it to be what it is. It's eight minutes long, it's. . . . The track had existed for a year already, but I just wanted to do something different with it. When I first started working on it, I was playing it out in the clubs on DAT, and someone heard it and said, "What is it? It sounds like you, the Art of Noise, and Aphex Twin all put together." I did a lot of sampling on it, like of my cat, some distortion, and some household things. And so when Trent came into the picture, we sent ADAT tapes back and forth, and kept on the phone during the process.

So Trent developed all the lyrics and melody lines?

Basically. . . . We're both artists, and when I work with the artist, I do my thing, and then I say, "I respect you as an artist. I dig what you do. So do what you do to this." It's kind of like, "Here's a painting. I'm not going to tell you what to do. Just do it." And what Trent did I thought was very cool. We actually did two different mixes of it. They did a mix and sent it to me, and then I did a mix, which is the one that ended up on the album. They made the vocals really stand out, like a song; like they're used to doing it. I'm used to dealing with it more like a track, where there's much more tension between the vocals and the track.

Speaking of samples, I hear other assorted "found sound" clips on this record. Tell us about some of these things.

The vocal thing from Sweet Pussy Pauline [on the song "Track 9"] was something sampled off her when she was in Philadelphia. That was kinda fun. She's a trip. Then there's "New Groove" which has a sample of my girlfriend Barbara and I talking about our first memories of water. It had to do with the whole texture thing again, and so there's a quick little vocal sample in there. We actually were out on the street one day miked up, and talking about our first memories of water as the cars were going by.

Once all of the elements of a song are recorded or sequenced, do you usually go for a mix immediately?

Sometimes I won't touch the desk for a week and just carry around a tape and listen to it again and again until I realize what will work. Sometimes it's just good to "bang out a track" and use that as a tool. Or I might press it up on a CD and play it out in a club. In terms of the dance music stuff, a lot of the vocal stuff obviously took more time because it's more like a song, and more thought had to go into it. I like thoughtless music, too, where whatever I feel — like an energy flow — just goes out, and it just grooves. I'm into that.

Music for the feet versus music for the head.

Exactly. But you could also just groove too, on like a bass line. You can hear this bass line forever and ever. And that's great. That's more or less a mistake theory, too. I never want to be able to discard something. Everything's always available to me. I never want to limit myself. I always want to be open for experiences of all sorts, like working with other musicians — opening up and having them learn from me and me learning from them. A lot of people like coming to the DJs, the whole DJ culture, to do remixes — remixers who are DJs. You know? Certain people need us, the DJs/remixers, now to get to a certain place, and that place is in the hands of the DJs at nightclubs and parties. I mean, a lot of the new Bowie and U2 stuff is looking toward the DJ and electronic culture for influences and or enthusiasm for their own music. Fripp is now doing some stuff. All these people, they've been involved in music for a long time — electronic music — but not necessarily so much on the dance side. [That type of music] may still be made for electronic musicians, but not for the dance floor and not for what's selling. And this is what's selling now.

How do you plan to recreate this music live?

What I want to do, instead of hauling all the gear and damaging it, is to end up just sampling certain bits. But I love to be able to tweak it. Especially the Roland [TB-]303 or something like that. A lot of people told me to check out [Steinberg] ReBirth. Novation has been great. I don't use Novation products to emulate a 303. I use them to do something totally different. Their filters and external inputs are great. You can use them as a tool. I'm still heavily into the 909 and 808 drum machines. I like them, but the Novation DrumStation is great for that. It's a rackmount, it's right there, you can tweak, as the pitch changes it writes it in, and it's awesome. That makes it great for a live show. But I'm in the midst of trying to sample everything I do, so for a live show I can bring an Akai MPC and a mixing desk with a hard drive for samples and consolidate my whole studio to three pieces of gear.

[by Greg Rule, Keyboard, October 1998]

Listening Guide

electronic music listening guide

Discs that Made a Difference

throughout these pages, our profiled artists have revealed their tools and techniques . . . their tricks and tips of the trade. For those of us who create electronic music, this makes for some stimulating shop talk, but ultimately the gadgets and gimmicks take a back seat to the final product: the music. In the big scheme of things, all the tools in the world are meaningless if the music doesn't move people.

Over the course of writing and editing this book, I sent invites to a variety of industry insiders (artists, critics, producers, and manufacturers) asking them to submit a list of their favorite or most influential electronic pop records of the past three decades.

What follows is the result of my email marathon . . . and a wide-ranging batch of submission they were. These are the CDs that our collective pool deemed worthy of space in your collection, listed in alphabetical order by artist. There are no doubt dozens of worthy artists who don't appear in this list, but consider this a good starting place.

• **Anderson, Laurie** *Big Science* (Warner Bros.). *Big Science* presaged big things to come from Anderson, a fixture in New York's alternative art scene. On this debut disc, she combined elements of Glass/Reich minimalism with the nihilistic feel and poetic adventurousness of Lou Reed. Her synth-heavy orchestrations were occasionally illuminated by bursts of unexpected sounds, including manipulated vocoder monologues, and, on one cut, bagpipes.

• **Aphex Twin** *Selected Ambient Works, Vols. 1 & 2, Classics* (Rough Trade). The mad scientist of electronica — Richard James — has been turning out wildly experimental and brilliant tracks throughout the '90s.

• **Art Of Noise** *Who's Afraid of . . . The Art of Noise* (Universal Records). A groundbreaking band who pre-dated a lot of what is going on now. Originally a studio project, the band was made up of synth greats Trevor Horn, Gary Langan, JJ Jeczalik, and Anne Dudley.

• **Beaver & Krause** *In a Wild Sanctuary* (Warner Bros.). Paul Beaver and Bernie Krause were among the few 1960s ambient pioneers who reached a pop audience. Paul has long since departed this plane, but Bernie was still producing ambient recordings as of this writing.

• **Björk** *Homogenic* (Elektra). Producer Mark Bell mixes his trash-truck electronic magic with Björk's soaring vocals on her third solo CD. Add the Icelandic String Quartet, and stand back. A stunning CD.

• **Bowie, David** *Low, Heroes* (Rykodisc). Groundbreaking ambient electronic work from one of pop's most enduring icons. "Bowie was a big influence during his *Low* period," says Nine Inch Nails mastermind Trent Reznor. "That was a big influence on *The Downward Spiral* from a point of, not only the mood and the desperation that it had, but structurally the songs are bizarre. One might not have any vocals, but you don't even realize it. You didn't even miss it."

• **Kate Bush** *The Dreaming* (EMI). Her fourth album won her new listeners around the world with its aggressive ethnic rhythms and swirling synth textures. Though guest shots by the likes of Geoff Downes on Fairlight sharpened the details of this hallucinogenic work, *The Dreaming* still thrusts you into an uncharted realm and won't let you escape.

• **Byrne/Eno** *My Life in the Bush of Ghosts* (Sire). Eno's collaboration with Talking Head David Byrne sent a jolt through the music world because of its use of spoken word samples in musical contexts. What would quickly become a cliché still sounds exciting here, with radio ranters and Arabian singers enhancing Byrne's slashing rhythms and Eno's electronic atmospheres. As Eno noted in *Keyboard's* July '81 issue, "On *My Life in the Bush of Ghosts* there's a very distinct collision of things. One is the collage technique, the found material technique. And that is, I think, very successfully united with a sort of rock-funk-African musical sensibility."

• **Carlos, Wendy** *Beauty in the Beast, Switched on Bach, A Clockwork Orange* (Columbia; reissues available on East Side Digital). *Beauty* was alternate tuning and additive synthesis at its absolute best. *Switched* was first album that showed that synthesizers could be real musical instruments; it held the "Best Selling Classical Album of All Time" title until 1975. *Clockwork*, a double album, included ground-

breaking experimental soundscapes that pre-dated the ambient music movement by at least a decade.

• **Chemical Brothers** *Dig Your Own Hole* (Astralwerks). One of the most lethal breakbeat-based records ever recorded. An explosion of acid synths and samples. Oasis's Noel Gallagher guests on the smash hit "Setting Sun."

• **Cibo Matto** *Viva La Woman* (Warner Bros.). Trippy, infectious loops and samples lay the foundation for one of the '90s most memorable pieces of electronic pop. Yuka Honda and Miho Hatori are the awesome twosome responsible for this delicious masterpiece.

• **Cirrus** *Drop the Break* (Moonshine). Hip-hop roots meet a rock mutation of Kraftwerk — and while synths, loops, and scratching are great, there's enough creative guitar work to prove that electronica needn't be a keyboards-only club.

• **Daft Punk** *Homework* (Virgin). Recorded in a bedroom studio, this high-profile debut has more hooks than a tackle shop. It's a feast of squelchy synths, funky beats, and vocoded vocals.

• **De Gaia, Banco** *Last Train To Lhasa* (Planet Dog/Mammoth). Leading British ambient technomeister Toby Marks was inspired by China's plans to build an unwanted railway across Tibet. *Last Train* exemplifies his intriguingly danceable soundscapes: the rich, layered, diverse works utilize all manner of Far Eastern exotica. Clocking in at a mere 35 minutes, "Kincajou (Duck! Asteroid)" is a recipe for hypnotism.

• **Depeche Mode** *Speak & Spell, Black Celebration, Violator, Songs of Faith & Devotion, Ultra* (Mute/Sire), *The Singles 81>85* and *86>98* (Reprise). The masters of minor keys, Depeche Mode are still selling out arenas and amphitheaters the world over. But surely no-one foresaw their Sire debut *Speak And Spell* (described as synthesized "bubble gum pop") leading to current world-domination status. *Black* was a turning point for the band, as they transitioned from a happier pop sound to the dark side. Their 1990s catalog *Violator, Songs Of Faith & Devotion* (studio and live versions), and *Ultra* earned them the title of undisputed stadium synth rock kings. The two *Singles* collections are a great overview of the band's career; both include bonus tracks.

• **Devo** *Q: Are We Not Men? A: We Are Devo.* (Warner Bros.). Their eccentric demolition of the Stones' "Satisfaction," along with brilliantly bizarre performances on "Jocko Homo" and "Mongoloid," pointed band-oriented listeners toward the emerging proto-techno world and established analog synths as a resource for garage bands suffering from guitar overdose.

• **Dolby, Thomas** *Golden Age of Wireless* (Capitol). Heavy MTV rotation of "She Blinded Me with Science" turned Dolby's first album into an unlikely sensation — unlikely because its filmy textures, obscure lyrics, and finely crafted tunes hardly fit the hit-making formula. Though Dolby's ear for synth arrangement was sharp even then, he had reservations about the album as a whole. "In order to get the record deal, l had to have the songs arranged and recorded as demos first," he told *Keyboard* in his Aug. '83 cover story. "So, in effect, when I did *Wireless*, all I was doing was recreating the demos, which isn't a good way of working."

• **Emerson, Lake & Palmer** *Brain Salad Surgery* (Atlantic). Classical meets electronics . . . this is a must for anyone looking to build a complete collection of historic synth recordings.

• **Eno, Brian** *Discrete Music, Music for Airports* (Caroline). *Discreet Music* paved the way, but *Airports* crystallized Eno's concept of stasis in sound and launched a thousand ships into ambient doldrums. Synth pop pioneer Vince Clarke said it all with this 1994 quote in *Keyboard*: "I quite like some ambient music when I hear it, although I don't know what I'm listening to. I did just rebuy Eno's *Music for Airports*."

• **Eno & Fripp** *No Pussyfooting* (Island). Frippertronic ambient guitar. High concept, low-budget loop-based trance music for the wannabe somnambulant artist in all of us.

• **Eurythmics** *Sweet Dreams Are Made of This* (BMG/RCA). This band was as stunning to look at as they were to listen to. Sporting a bright orange buzzcut and a business suit, singing sensation Annie Lennox teamed with multi-instrumentalist Dave Stewart and set the pop music world on fire. Stewart appeared on the cover of *Keyboard* in 1984, and in his interview revealed that the song was made on a Teac 8-track recorder.

• **Foxx, John** *Metamatic* (Virgin). Ultravox's founder John Foxx unleashed an almost all-synthesized collage of drum machines and tape-based rhythm loops. No cymbals and few chords were used. Foxx stripped the music back to functional essentials — proto-techno, in effect.

• **Gabriel, Peter** *So* (Geffen). Gabriel is a virtuoso conceptualist with the gift of applying his resources to their fullest extent in service of an adventurous idea, and *So* is perhaps his crowning achievement. This collection of songs, most of them basic in structure, was brought to life through an inspired fusion of emotion and technology. Gabriel's synth parts lead the opening cut, "Red Rain," from the slightest of introductions through furious peaks and back down to a simple triadic finish. Throughout the album the dominant textures derive from a Fairlight CMI and a Sequential Prophet-5, with bits of Yamaha CS-80 thrown in now and then, yet the expression Gabriel wrings from these tools is extraordinary.

• **Hammer, Jan** *The First Seven Days* (Nemperor). At age 28, Hammer was already recognized as one of the most exciting live synth players through his work with Mahavishnu Orchestra when he hung up his stage clothes, disappeared into his home studio, and created this early example of a one-man synth album. With Moog, Oberheim, and Freeman synths, a Mellotron, and electric and acoustic pianos, he composed and performed a powerful programmatic tour de force, arranged to evoke the story of Genesis (the Biblical, not English, one).

• **Hancock, Herbie** *Future Shock* (Columbia). With so many terrific Hancock albums released over the decades, *Future Shock* stands out because it best represents Hancock's fearless attitude toward genre jumping. It took guts for a master of jazz harmony and subtle soloing to jump this deep into the synthesized fray. But for all the turntable scratches and hip-hop affectations, Hancock's spare yet irresistible funky synth and Clav work

are what make *Future Shock* sound fresh to this day.

• **Hassell, Jon** *Earthquake Island* (Tomato). Combining elements of jazz, Asian, African, Eastern, and South American music, Hassell's approach to electronic music was like no other. A student of electro legend Karlheinz Stockhausen, Hassell rewrote music history with breakthrough solo efforts and collaborations with Talking Heads, Brian Eno, and Daniel Lanois.

• **Human League,** *The Greatest Hits* (Virgin). If you have room for only one Human League disc in your collection, this is the one to get. It's wall-to-wall hits, and all packed with catchy vocals and analog synth lines. About their biggest hit of all, "Don't You Want Me," Philip Oakley told *Keyboard* in 1982 that "the horn sound has a lot of string parts in it that are a mixture of pizzicato strings and horns. I think it's a really good sound, and one that's never been on record before." And a sound that was copied for years after.

• **Japan** *Gentlemen Take Polaroids/ Tin Drum/Oil on Canvas* box set (Caroline). Another group who made big inroads to the '80s. With David Sylvian at the controls and cool spin-offs from Mick Karn as well as drummer Steve Jansen (Sylvian's estranged brother), and keyboardist Richard Barbieri, they set new standards for much of the electro/neo romantica of the era.

• **Jarre, Jean-Michel** *Oxygene* (Polydor). An infectious combination of bouncy, bubbling analog sequences and memorable hook lines. Top French export Jean-Michel Jarre crafted *Oxygene* carefully over four months in his eight-track studio. Tracks fade in and out behind Mellotron pads and evocations of chirping birds, guiros, and breathing. Yet *Oxygene* was designed with live performance in mind. "I want to be able to do the music by myself on tour and have it sound just like it did in the studio," he told *Keyboard* in 1978.

• **KMFDM** *Retro* (TVT/Wax Trax). A retrospective collection from one of Germany's most hard-hitting and influential industrial ensembles. Put on a football helmet for this one.

• **Kraftwerk** *Computer World Trans-Europe Express* (EMI/Elektra). It's been claimed that this German band rewrote the future; possibly the most revered electronic music group of all time, and it's easy to see why. *Computer World*, their eerily prophetic landmark, taught today's young techno pretenders a thing or too. Stylistically light years ahead of its competition. And while you're at it, be sure to snap up a copy of the highly-influential *Trans-Europe Express* (reissues available on Cleopatra Records).

• **Madonna** *Ray of Light* (Maverick). One of the highest-profile collaborations in electronic-pop history. Ambient pioneer William Orbit takes the megastar singer to new synthesized heights.

• **Marilyn Manson** *Antichrist Superstar* (Nothing/Interscope). Dig beyond the shock-rock layer of this band and you'll find some amazing synth and computer work.

• **Massive Attack** *Mezzanine* (Virgin). Trip-hop at its finest. Critics the world over deemed this one of the top discs of 1998. A perfect marriage of cutting edge electronic productions and pop melodies.

• **Masters At Work** *NuYorican Soul* (Giant Step). Little Louie Vega and Kenny Dope bring together an all-star lineup of musical talent on this breakthrough CD: from Tito Puente and Eddie Palmieri to Jocelyn Brown and George Benson.

• **Meat Beat Manifesto** *Subliminal Sandwich* (Nothing/Interscope). Jack Dangers doesn't just make music; on this stunning CD he creates a whole jungle ecosystem. The atmosphere is thick and steamy, the sounds oddly organic, and the path twists and turns until you loose all sense of direction. Wild.

• **Miles, Robert** *Dreamland* (Arista). Get this CD if for no other reason than to hear the global phenomenon called "Children." Written as a chill-out theme for European raves, this track was one of the most influential hybrids of gentle piano melodies and pulsing techno.

• **Morcheeba** *Big Calm* (Sire). Cast this one in the same light as Portishead, Massive Attack, and Sneaker Pimps. World-class trip-hop.

• **Nine Inch Nails** *Pretty Hate Machine* (TVT), *Broken, The Downward Spiral* (Nothing/Interscope). Take your pick. These industrial-strength masterpieces are about as in-your-face as electronic music gets. Samplers meet distortion boxes — no one does industrial better.

• **Numan, Gary** *Tubeway Army, Replicas* (Beggars Banquet). Post-punk, skeletal, analog electronica by British synth pop pioneer Gary Numan. The dreamily epic "Down in the Park" and Europe-wide vanguard monster hit "Are Friends Electric?" arguably opened the floodgates for the early '80s wave of electronic acts to follow. Undeniably a classic.

• **Pet Shop Boys** *Please, Alternative* (EMI). Hailing from London, Chris Lowe and Neil Tennant are perhaps best known for their chart-topping single "West End Girls." A synth-intensive sensation, the song was no overnight success. Initially released in 1984, it racked up mild numbers in the States, but failed to get much attention back home. When Stephen Hauge assisted in a remixed version nearly two years later, though, the song broke through on both sides of the Atlantic. *Please* is the record that started it all, while *Alternative* is the eclectic collection of B-sides.

• **Photek** *Modus Operandi* (Astralwerks). Rupert Parkes, one of the undisputed masters of drum 'n' bass music, fuses his '70s jazz fusion, Detroit techno, and soundtrack-like sensibilities with cutting edge electronics, and the results are mesmerizing. His tracks are a lesson in intricacy.

• **Pink Floyd** *Pipers at the Gates of Dawn* (Capitol). Syd Barrett and later the other guys in the band really started a trend toward more electronica in

pop music. Later records like *Meddle, Wish You Were Here,* and *Animals,* while not techno dance stuff per se, definitely led the way toward this increasing trend to favor the electro side of things in pop music.

• **Portishead** *Dummy* (London/Polygram). This is the dark, melancholic disc from Bristol that changed the music world. Lo-fi and spy movie motifs meet grainy loops and pop melodies. Awesome.

• **Prodigy** *Fat of the Land* (Maverick). The media frenzy surrounding this CD in 1997 was unprecedented . . . and justified. Infectious hooks meet masterful hi-tech productions.

• **Propellerheads** *Decksndrumsnrocknroll* (Dreamworks). Fierce, wildly energetic music that's guaranteed to make even the most faint pulse pound.

Watching this talented duo live is even more breathtaking.

• **Residents** *Meet the Residents* (East Side Digital). Called "true avant-garde crazies" by the UBL Web site, the Residents took the weird world of found sounds, beat boxes, and lo-brow electronics to bold new highs . . . and lows.

• **Saunders, Jesse** *Chicago Reunion: The Pioneers of House Music* (Broken Records). This double-CD package is a history lesson of sorts, with dialog between the tracks explaining the birth of Chicago house music.

• **Size, Roni** *New Forms* (Polygram). A pioneer of drum 'n' bass, Roni Size set the world on fire with this masterful cut/paste collage.

• **Skinny Puppy** *Rabies, 12-inch Anthology* (Nettwerk Records). One of electronic music's most hard-edged and influential bands.

• **Sneaker Pimps** *Becoming X, Becoming Remixed* (Virgin). One of the most memorable trip-hop CDs since Portishead's classic debut. And don't miss the excellent follow-up CD of remixes, featuring Armand Van Helden's classic reworking of "Spin, Spin Sugar."

• **Tangerine Dream** *Poland* (Castle Communications). Prolific Teutonic techno godfathers . . . . Tangerine Dream's 20-plus-year commitment to the technological cutting edge is admirable. *Poland* was recorded live in Cold War-torn Warsaw. A slow, moody, West-meets-Eastern-bloc intro moves on to a Polish electronic jig climax, with peaceful choral interludes and a pseudo-Ennio Morricone theme, possibly inspired by founder Edgar Froese's appreciation of the Western film genre.

• **Think Tank** *Skullbuggery* (Hakatak International). Nonstop creative sound design in a hard-driving techno format. Dialog samples provide a multidimensional commentary on the man-machine culture, and the beats just keep on pumpin'.

• **Tomita, Isao** *The Planets* (RCA). During their novelty years in the 1970s, synthesizers planted themselves in the public ear mainly as sources of sci-fi space effects or gee-whiz tools for replicating orchestral instruments. Some early synthesists combined the two approaches, and none did so with as much repeated success as this Tokyo-based composer.

• **Vangelis** *China* (Polygram), *Heaven and Hell* (Windham Hill). This Greek magician has of late been confined to audiences of more "new age" types, but in case you haven't heard his early experiments, check them out. The pop electro music of today would not be at all where it is without him, no doubt.

• **Various Artists** *MTV AMP 1 & II* compilations (Astralwerks). All-star compilations featuring tracks by Aphex Twin, Crystal Method, Chemical Brothers, Photek, Prodigy, Underworld, Josh Wink, Air, Fatboy Slim, Goldie, Propellerheads, Roni Size, and more.

[**Contributors: Jim Aikin, Craig Anderton, Candy Chan, Vince Clarke, Paul Craven, Robert L. Doerschuk, Joey Donatello, Mikail Graham, Ted Greenwald, Chris Grigg, John Krogh, Brian McNelis, Dominic Milano, Jonathan Miller, Trent Reznor, Greg Rule, Kylé Swenson]**

about the author

Greg Rule is an associate editor at *Keyboard* magazine, and a recording artist. He's remixed songs by Faith No More, the Fixx, KMFDM, Sister Machine Gun, Electric Hellfire Club, Manfred Mann, and others, and his electronic dance tracks can be heard on a series of Hypnotic Records compilations. Greg supplied the samples and drum beats for Kawasaki's musical toy Big Bam Boom, and he scored the subsequent TV commercial spots. He is a voting member of NARAS, the National Academy of Recording Arts & Sciences.

acknowledgments

(m) any thanks to those who helped make this book possible. . . .

Jim Aikin, Doug Beck, Jennie Boddy, Candy Chan, Dorothy Cox, Tom Darter, Robert L. Doerschuk, Joey Donatello, Billy Gould, Mikail Graham, Debbie Greenberg, Ted Greenwald, Jan Hughes, Tonya Hurley, Matt Kelsey, Costa Kotselas, Jerry Kovarsky, John Krogh, May Lam, Neil Lawi, Rich Leeds, Brian McNelis, Dominic Milano, Jonathan Miller, Mike Molenda, Bob Moog, Ernst Nathorst, Jim Norris, Marvin Sanders, Robert Semrow, Kylé Swenson, the Ultimate Band List (www.ubl.com), Mark Vail, Howard Wuelfing, and Sioux Z.

artist index